The Artist's Survival Guide

What They Never Taught You in School

James Barbour

ISBN Hardback: 978-1-951503-31-4
ISBN Softback: 978-1-951503-30-7

TABLE OF CONTENTS

PART I: MINDSET

Part II: Marketing

PREFACE
READ THIS NOW

You will fail.

You'll never make it. It's too hard. You'll be a waiter your entire life. You'll give up. Make sure you have something to fall back on. Get a real job. You don't want to be another starving artist.

Have you heard any of these phrases? They are the frequent mutterings of those around us advising us on what they think will be the outcome of pursuing our dreams. They are even the internal thoughts and doubts that creep into our minds—they are the words we sometimes tell ourselves.

You need to remove these words, these people, and these thoughts from your life immediately. Cut them out like a cancer and never let them in again. You can confront this reality or ignore it. Confronting it will set you on a path toward your dreams, ignoring it will lead you down the path of failure.

The choice is yours.

I've spent my life creating art. I've hit great heights and fallen to great depths, yet I'm still here. I'm still going and I'm still working at a high level. It doesn't matter who you are, or what you have or have not accomplished. It doesn't matter if you've hit roadblocks, pitfalls, hit the bottom, hit heights—it doesn't matter the color of your skin, your religious or non-religious beliefs, if you feel you're too old, that you're the "wrong" gender, and so on. *It doesn't matter*. Turn off the noise! Stop listening to those who say you can't or you never will. Stop listening to the self-doubt. With the right tools, you have a chance to make your dreams a reality.

The choice is yours.

In the following chapters I shed light on some of those tools and how to use them. If you truly want to "make it" as a professional artist, then make a commitment to yourself to remove all preconceived notions, opinions, and negative thoughts. The path I lay out in this book may not be the only way, but it IS a way and it's been proven. What are you going to do?

The choice is yours.

If you're still reading, then chances are you have something unique within you that refuses to stay silent—a burning desire that is pushing you to create, to make a difference in the world with your vision. Whether you're a singer, actor, fine artist, fashion designer, photographer, musician, dancer, filmmaker, writer, or even if you have an artist hidden somewhere within you with a fire inside that refuses to go out, then I hope the words in this book can help you to unleash your star power and make your dream a reality.

Perhaps that fire has dwindled to a spark, but it does indeed remain inside. It might be dormant, covered by the ash of doubt and unfulfilled promises, but that ember still glows. All you need to do is breathe some air on it and in no time it will reignite into a full flame shining the light on your ultimate dream once again.

It is true that the life of an artist is one fraught with obstacles, objections, rejections, and criticisms. But if you are a real artist of any sort, then somewhere deep within your soul you have an unquenchable thirst, a drive, a passion to create, and that fire inside. Know this. Hold it strong because if you want to succeed in this industry, you'll need that light burning so bright that it blocks out everything pushing you away from achieving what you truly want. The doubts, the naysayers, the "you're-not-good-enoughs," the "you can'ts," and the "you never wills" will be daunting obstacles. You'll need to see clearly what you are facing and drive forward within your passion to become a thriving artist.

Here's a caveat: If you're afraid of hard work and fear you won't make it as a professional artist, then this book isn't for you. The information here isn't sugar-coated. You won't be looking through rose colored glasses or getting a slap on the back just because you played the lead in your high school musical or because your parents think you take great photographs. Instead, this book lays out some cold hard facts about surviving as a professional artist. This is a raw and very direct look at the reality of life as an artist and how you can put tools in place to help you reach your goals.

I've broken the book into two main sections, Mindset and Marketing. Mindset is the first section and deals with the truths of the professional artist. It's preparation for the second section, Marketing, which is all about the tools needed to break free of the chains that have been holding you down.

The information contained in this book comes from my nearly forty years of working as a professional artist at the highest level in my field. I've lived it, worked it, learned what to do and what not to do, met obstacles and challenges along the way, and continue to thrive in what many would consider one of the most difficult professions in the world even when there were those who counted me out.

If you want to stay safe, feel comfortable, and keep the embers buried and hidden within you, then please pass this book on to someone who truly wants to break free and create their dream.

No one is going to give you a handout. No one is going to "make you a star." You've got to put in the work. If you truly want to take your career to the next level, then you've got to put in the work. If you want to do what thousands of people only dream of doing, then you've got to put in the work. If you're ready to meet the challenges and rise to greater heights within yourself, then buckle up!

The choice is yours.

INTRODUCTION
2020, THE YEAR THE EARTH STOOD STILL

Everyone will remember the year 2020. It was the year of the Coronavirus. It was the year that the Earth Stood Still. It is the first year in 115 years that all movie theaters closed their doors, Broadway shows completely shut down, television and film production instantly stopped, and the entertainment industry came to a grinding halt. No jobs for actors or technicians, no concerts for singers or musicians, no live performances, no art exhibitions…nothing. The income and livelihood of almost every creative artist I know dried up instantly.

The reality is that life as an artist was bleak and sketchy even before 2020. But the COVID-19 Pandemic put that uncertainty on an even more unstable foundation. Questions abounded about how to survive, how to make ends meet, pay bills, pay rent, feed the family. The irony, if there is any irony in all of this, is that these are questions artists have always faced, but now they face *every artist simultaneously*.

Understand the gravity of this. The downtime was not staggered. Normally there is a staggered, almost layered reality to being an out-of-work artist where some would be employed while others weren't. It was a normal cycle. But in 2020 everyone was hit at the same time and almost every art-

"

ist I know was instantly out of work at the same time. They became dependent on the "system" to take care of them, relying on unemployment, government subsidies, and whatever they had in savings. Support systems such as these will eventually run out. There will eventually be no more unemployment, no more subsidies, and no more savings. Without money coming in and only money going out the well will inevitably run dry.

With everyone being affected simultaneously, these once singular questions of survival have now risen to the forefront of every artist on the planet at the same time.

Scary.

I've been advising artists to take a serious look at these things for years—things like how to survive between gigs, how to create residual streams of income independent of your work as an artist, and how to create a brand that allows you the freedom of not relying on others for your success.

These questions are even more relevant today. The answers are vital to your survival, and not just as an artist—they are vital to your survival, period.

Let me ask you a couple of questions, and I want you to answer them honestly:

- If you had enough money to cover every one of your expenses on a continual basis with surplus left over, how would you feel during the "down times?"

- If you had enough money to continually cover your expenses, how would you feel if your current artistic gig ended?

- If you had enough money to continually cover your bills, would you be stressed about your unemployment check running out?

If you had planted seeds earlier that you could harvest in the lean times, you could very well be in a situation where money was not an issue. You would be able to navigate the rough waters and most importantly make the artistic choices you *want* to make based on your artistic ideals and not be dependent on taking each and every gig that came down the pike just to make ends meet. You would be in the driver's seat. You would be more in control.

Make no mistake, the year of 2020 impacted the world in a way never before experienced. The earth truly did stand still and in response to this wake-up call you need to look at your life as an artist the same way a businessperson looks at their business. Remember, it's not called Show Show, it's called Show *Business*. It's time to dig in, look, learn, and grow.

WHY?

When I embarked on a career as an actor, I didn't have anyone to advise me or guide me. I didn't have a road map into the arts and entertainment industry. I didn't go to a "conservatory school," didn't have an agent, manager, or lawyer. I moved to New York City with no connections. I wasn't part of any union. I knew no one and no one knew me. It was like setting forth into uncharted territory using only the stories and fables I had heard along the way as guideposts. Yet I was focused, driven, and dedicated. Those negative phrases I mentioned in the opening section of the book hit me as they did everyone else, but somehow I deflected them. Perhaps I was too naive, optimistic, innocent, wide-eyed, who knows. But one thing is for certain, I *never* let those words stop me...*ever*.

Oh they flew around me like leaves in a storm. I was aware of them and I heard others talking about them all the time, but I never let them penetrate my being. I worked, I learned, I built, and I grew. In fact, I used them as fuel. Whenever I would hear someone second-guessing my goals, talents, or abilities, I would use that as a catalyst. I was going to prove them wrong. The more I heard them, the more determined I became.

I can remember only three times in my life when I was told to my face I didn't have what it takes to make it in the industry. One was by a high school teacher and the other was by an agent. The third time was early in my career when a prominent director told my agents that he just didn't "get me." Funny thing…that teacher later became my biggest supporter, that agent became my first agent, and although I never worked with that director, after his comment I went on to star in multiple Broadway shows with many of the same creative people he had worked with over the years.

The truth, statistically speaking, is that they're correct. The vast majority of people entering into the entertainment industry fail. They give up their artistic dream and choose another profession.

But rather than succumb to the power of people, words, ideas, and statistics, those people, those words, those ideas, and those statistics pushed me, drove me to prove them wrong. I learned how to navigate the business through trial and error (otherwise known as the school of hard knocks), and I have the scars to prove it.

I never starved, I never went homeless, and have made my income almost exclusively from performance. In fact, I only held two non-arts-related jobs in my professional life, and both of those were when I first got to New York City. Come to think of it, the first one was actually dealing with the world of Broadway.

That first job was selling Broadway tickets to theatre patrons. I would call people from a list of qualified prospects, pitching them (usually during their dinner hour) on purchasing tickets to shows. This was a great job because it was in the very industry I was trying to break into, but it had nothing to do with performance.

I sucked at that job. I mean I *really* sucked. I was cold calling people during their dinner hour out of the blue. More often than not I would end up chatting with the prospect about a show they recently saw or apologizing for interrupting their dinner. I knew deep down this job wasn't for me. My focus was on performing. During the day I pounded the pavement until I was finally cast in a regional theatre gig, and promptly left that sales job.

The second job was working at a place called Hackers, Hitters and Hoops—at that time the only indoor batting cages in Manhattan. This was a fun job and within a couple of weeks I was asked to be one of the managers. The problem here was that I could feel this job pulling me away from my dream. I was making some money, it was a fun place, and I got to meet some great people including the actor Jerry O'Connell. He would come in with his friends to use the batting cages on a frequent basis. I'm eight years older than Jerry, but even at this point he already had a massive career having starred in movies like *Stand by Me*, which had come out about five years earlier.

I remember him being a very nice guy—very personable and upbeat. We would chat when he was there and one day, knowing I was an actor, he asked if I was going to Los Angeles for "pilot season." I had no answer. I had no answer because I didn't even know what pilot season was. I certainly wasn't going, and I felt a bit of a letdown inside. What was I missing? This was a freaking wake up call. I was living in New York, working at Hackers, Hitters and Hoops, auditioning during the day, but I wasn't living my dream. I wasn't playing the game at the right level. I was being complacent. It was then and there that I made the decision. The next day I gave my two weeks' notice and never looked back.

Success in the world of art and artists is usually based on the Alpha and the Omega—those who have risen to stardom, and those who have given up. Like I shared earlier, those negating comments swirled everywhere in the industry. It's like being in LA—you can't cross your legs without hitting an actor or writer or filmmaker, all of whom are quick to share their big dreams floating on a sea of self-importance. I realized that the self-aggrandizing, self-important air was often covering self-doubt, fear, and insecurity because of the harsh reality we as artists face. I slowly became numb to it, and it eventually became fuel pushing me forward. You have a dream, a goal that is within you. If you've contemplated this path, then you've probably had visions of being both the Alpha and the Omega—stardom and failure.

In truth there is a huge bracket in between the two. There is only one Lady Gaga, one Rock, one Robert Downey Jr., one Donna Karan, one Andy Warhol…you get the picture. Will you reach that level of success? Maybe, maybe not. That level of stardom and influence is extremely rare. Nonetheless you have that drive, that goal, that undefinable "thing" that pushes you forward. To attain it you need to focus and endure. You must work diligently on your career if you want to break through the barriers and be a professional, to be someone who is self-sustaining solely as an artist.

So why have I written this book?

I wrote this book to provide you with that which I never had—a road map, a survival guide for one of the toughest professions there is. I've spoken to countless artists driven by their dreams, yet who are lost when it comes to surviving long enough in this field to make those dreams a reality. How do you get there? What do you do?

If you take a trip of any length, you always use navigation tools. These tools have changed over the centuries from plotting star charts, using compasses and maps, to navigation apps on your phone. We have been and still are relying on some sort of map to guide us toward our destination. Even on short trips we use markers to identify where to go. These can be as simple as a street sign, a stop light, or an exit number on a highway, yet you are always using an identifiable piece of information to help you determine your path.

Without a road map or navigation tool you can become lost and begin to wander on your path. Best case scenario is you'll get there with no problems, but more often you'll be delayed in reaching your goal, and the worst-case scenario is never reaching it at all. Having a road map is essential. Being too proud to use one is costly and amateurish.

As professional artists we know the "traditional" ways to get to where we want to go. We've seen them, observed them, been told "this is how you do things." As actors, for example, this includes getting into class, auditioning, finding an agent, manager, lawyer, a press rep to help us move to the next level, and ultimately booking a gig that will lead to the next better gig, and so on. Singer/songwriters write, perform, record, and submit their work to anyone and everyone who can possibly hear it, get them a deal, buy their song, etc.

No matter what type of artist you are, there is "a way" that it's always been done, and that's the way most of us have chosen to follow. Why?

Because no one has shown you or taught you that there are alternatives.

Dreams without action are just dreams. You must take action in order to accomplish something. A great mindset is wonderful, but without action behind that positivity you'll be a positive person who has not achieved their goal. *Action creates traction.*

There is a famous, often misquoted poem by Robert Frost called "The Road Not Taken." Most people mistakenly refer to it as "The Road Less Traveled," but stated either way it has been interpreted by many people over the years. The phrase is used to encourage people to cut their own path, blaze their own trail, and while I love this sentiment, there is a time and a place for that and it's not always the right choice. Here's what I mean:

You're in a dense jungle rain forest and you need to get through that jungle to the city on the other side. Directly in front of you is thick, overgrown jungle, but to the side of that jungle is a well-worn dirt path which leads directly to the city. What do you do? Do you take the existing road or The Road Not Taken? You can certainly cut your own path or blaze your own trail through the jungle, face unforeseen challenges, hack through the brush and trees, avoid wild animals, swamps, and who knows what else. At the very least, even if there aren't any major obstacles, it will certainly take you a lot longer to cut your way through the jungle than it would to take the worn path. Either path you take, you will still have to put in the work to get there by walking, running, riding, driving, etc.

There is certainly value in learning how to cut your way through obstacles (the school of hard knocks), but are these the obstacles from which you wish to learn? What is your priority? Remember the goal. The goal above is to get to the city on the other side. Your goal is to succeed as a professional artist. If you want to overcome obstacles, then focus on overcoming the challenges within your art. Become a better actor, painter, filmmaker, dancer. Do not focus on things that will distract you from your goal. If you have a way to get to your destination, your goal, your dream, faster and with less bumps and bruises, then you should take it!

Take the road *more* traveled to achieve your goal. Once you've reached it you can then take the lessons you've learned along the way to now set off and blaze a trail of your own… and perhaps, this time, people will follow *you*.

PART I

MINDSET

WHAT IF?

What if you won $200 million in the lottery? I want you to list out all the things you would do if you won that money. Close your eyes and envision it. Feel it. $200 million in your bank account…right now. Grab a notebook or piece of paper and write them down. Would you pay off debt, student loans, buy a house, pay off your house, help a family member, make a film, an album, open an art gallery, quit everything and go on vacation forever? Kind of cool, right? Money in this sense creates freedom.

That feeling of freedom is what you need in your life, and moreover it's what you need in your *creative* life. You can create that mindset of success and apply it to your current situation even though you don't have the $200 million in the bank. You didn't have the money when you visualized the possibilities, and yet those possibilities were and are real. You just need to put action behind them.

What if your dreams came true? What if you reach your goals? What if you find the perfect partner, the perfect house, what if you could find eternal happiness? What if you could have everything you've always wanted? What's the worst thing that could happen?

I want to help you do is to create that same feeling of freedom as an artist so you have a better chance of achieving whatever goal you choose to visualize. Putting the dream into action is where most everyone gets stuck.

As we all know, the chances of winning the lottery are very unlikely. You have a better chance of betting on *yourself*. If you do the work, put in the hours and plan, you *can* achieve what you put your mind to.

So think about it. What if you truly could have everything you've always wanted? It's possible. It just takes work.

Grab a notebook and follow along.

These are the beginning steps to you creating *your* personal Artist's Survival Guide.

I'm listing four steps I've used successfully in my life and career that have given me clarity and focus to achieve many wonderful things. I'm going to be referring to these at various times throughout the book, and they will come into play as each chapter of the book, your life, and your career unfolds.

THE 4 STEPS

STEP 1: IDENTIFY

Identify your purpose. What do you want to do? What is your dream, your ultimate goal? I want you to write it down. Write down the absolute dream goal you've had in the back of your mind your entire life. It's the thing that gives you a sense of joy and happiness—the thing that when you're quiet with yourself makes your heart beat with excitement. While you're contemplating this, I want to also put this into your mind: Grant Cardone is a New York Times best-selling author and a massively successful entrepreneur who has taught me an incredible amount about creating and manifesting wealth and success. He said something which rang so true to me and I'm going to share it with you. He said this: If you're tired all the time, if you don't have enough energy to do your job, then you're doing the wrong job.

The thing that excites you, motivates you, that you would work on 24/7 is *the* thing that you should be doing. It's your purpose. That's what I want you to find in yourself. Do not edit yourself, do not filter your choices because of things you've been told, this is *your* purpose, *your* goal. Find it, then write it down no matter what it is.

STEP 2: CONFRONT

Confront the reality of where you are in your life. This is always a hard thing to do because you have to be completely truthful with yourself. Look at your finances, look at your skill level, look at the competition in your field, even look at your geographical location. Look at *everything* in your life and confront those things you've been avoiding or sweeping under the rug. Write them down.

This step might take a little bit of time, and you can add to it as you go, but trust me here, once everything is out in the open, once the cards are laid bare, you'll be able to move forward with the next steps more easily.

STEP 3: REMOVE

Remove any obstacles you find standing in the way of achieving your success. It can be as simple as removing bad foods from your refrigerator, or perhaps something more difficult such as removing negative people from your life. The latter is a bit trickier but make no mistake, removing the natters, gossipers, haters, and naysayers will do wonders for your outlook, stability, and purpose. It will also do incredible things for your productivity. You won't have anchors hanging around your neck holding you down, dragging you to the bottom of the ocean. You'll move faster, cleaner, and with no negativity weighing you down.

Write these down and take no prisoners. This is a vital step. If you have unhealthy foods in your house, then you'll be more tempted to eat them, but if you remove them and don't buy them, then they won't be there to tempt you. The same is true of negative influences.

You might come across something you can't immediately remove. Here's an example: You want to be in a Broadway show, but you live and work in Virginia. Moving immediately to New York might not be a reality for you at the moment but it *is* something you'll want to do if you want to make a go of it on Broadway. Just like someone who lives in Minnesota and wants to study the tropical fish of Hawaii. They're really not going to be able to do that at the highest level unless they go to Hawaii. You get the picture. If you want to compete and make it in your chosen field, then you *must* do everything you can possibly do to give yourself the best shot. So even though the move might not be immediately possible, write it down (and anything else that might fall into this category) and keep it as something to address.

I also want you to use this step to think outside the box. I want you to use this to remove any negative thoughts you might have about yourself, your skill sets, and your current condition. Write them down.

Once it's on paper, then it's in your battle plan of attack and is now part of your journey.

STEP 4: ADD AND INCREASE

Add to and increase those things that are moving you **toward** your goals. These might be things like honing your skills in your chosen field (dancing, singing, acting, learning more about photography, paint and canvas, writing, cinematography, etc.). Study everything you can and learn as much as possible about your field. It also includes spending time with supportive friends, eating and sleeping better, and something

I consider *very* important: Keep your lines open to those who motivate you.

The reason I've put these four steps in at this point is because you need to have a clean approach to your life. If you want to create stability in your career, if you want to expand beyond the limitations imposed upon you by the "outside" world, then you must remove those limitations you've put on yourself. You'll need clarity and focus to take control of the wheel because you'll be driving all of it.

THE LAUNCHPAD

Every successful person I know is connected to and/ or studies with a coach or mentor of some sort. I am constantly reading, learning and studying from anyone I can possibly learn from. My examples are Grant Cardone (whose training I use on a consistent basis), Ted McGrath (who has been vital to helping me grow my businesses), and Tim Storey (who has become a great friend and life coach). I try to learn from anyone who can help me grow as an artist, in business, and as a person.

You may notice, if you know them, that the people I've mentioned above are not "artists" in the traditional sense. I didn't list actors or singers or directors. There's a reason for this. I had and still have artists who I admire, including Anthony Hopkins, Gary Oldman, Lisa Harrow, Alejandro González Iñarrítu, Salvador Dalí, and the list goes on and on. These are the artists whose work inspires me. I use them as templates and "mentors" for my art, but not for the *business* of art. Remember, we are coming at this from a different viewpoint. You already know *how* to create your art, the questions we are answering here is how to *survive* while doing it!

Ask yourself this: "How am I going to take my skill and make a living from it? How do I get my art, my skill set, my craft, and myself exposure in the industry, to people and, dare I say it, to the world? How am I going to monetize what

I do so my art doesn't sit in a vacuum? How am I going to be in complete control of my career and income?

As an artist, heck in any profession or walk of life, *you are your product.* The people I follow have been able to take their product and create something bigger than themselves. They've created movements behind them, cultures behind them, and as such their work, their product, their art is now accessible to millions of people *worldwide.* And then what do they do? They leverage that visibility to create even more. That, to me, is the name of the game. I want to effect positive change on the world through my art and what I do. The way to do that is by reaching as many people as possible.

Remember, your skill, your art, your abilities, are all things that you *must* have in place and continue to grow. But you must also find a way to expand and grow so your skill, your art, and your abilities reach more people. People who are influential in their fields are so because they've proven what they do has impact. They've created a situation in their lives and careers where they have become "stars," whether in the entertainment field or not. Richard Branson, Donna Karan, Oprah, The Dali Lama, Elon Musk, Grant Cardone, J.K. Rowling...you get the picture.

By following and learning from those who have created massive growth and applying your personal skill set as an artist to the paths these people have taken, you marry the best of both worlds. A professional artist must understand and know business. One cannot exist without the other.

I'm going to say this again, it's not called Show Show, it's called Show *Business.*

If no one buys your art, if no one sees your art, then you're creating in a vacuum. You need to expand, you need to grow, and the way to do that is by implementing some basic principles for success.

One major key to success is finding someone who has become successful in the field you're in and literally study what they did to achieve their success. They *did* something to get there, they took steps, so why not learn what they did and do the same thing? They've laid the path for you. They've created a road map to success.

Obviously, everyone's journey will be different and each of us is unique. But as far as I'm concerned, if someone lays down a road map to success, then I'm going to follow it. I might drive that road a little differently, in a different vehicle, and I might hit a detour now and then, but at least with a map I'm not driving blindly.

Professional vs Amateur

If you want to compete in the world of art you must have a skill set, and that skill set needs to be continually honed because the competition is fierce. To play in the NBA or NFL you need to have skill, and if you don't then you'll be run over, literally. These elite athletes are professionals, and the most successful of these pros are focused on the actions that will make them the best in their game… continually. What would happen if you took those seasoned professionals and put them up against a team of amateurs who only played the sport as a pastime? It wouldn't be pretty.

It's vitally important to your future as an artist to understand the difference between a professional and an amateur.

A common way to define the word "professional" is one who is "engaged in a specified activity as one's main paid occupation rather than as a pastime."

An "amateur" can be defined as "a person who engages in a pursuit, especially a sport, on an unpaid rather than a professional basis." The word can also be used to mean "a person who is incompetent or inept at a particular activity."

Does every professional make enough money to survive out of the gate? Certainly not. Professional vs amateur is as much a mindset as it is a reality, but the actions you put behind that mindset matter. When you take up the mantle of a pro, you must live, act, make decisions, study, and plan like a professional. Only then have you begun. When you hesitate, question, second-guess, and delay, then you are taking the road of an amateur. I remember a martial arts teacher telling me that once you've achieved your black belt, only then you are truly a student. Get that? After all the years of work and dedication, class after class, belt after belt. Only when you achieve your black belt are you truly a student. Not a master…a *student*.

And let me be clear here: There's nothing wrong with being an amateur artist, nothing at all. Not everyone can be a professional, but there is a vast difference between the two.

So which are you? Decide now because the two are like oil and water when it comes to surviving as an artist…they simply don't mix. As a professional you will need to make hard, tough choices that will determine your trajectory and your future. If you're an amateur then you will never have to make some of the life-altering decisions you would as a pro.

Choosing life as an artist isn't a vacation, it's not play time, it's real, it's hard, and it *is* a business. Make no mistake about that. It is a hard-fought battle against yourself, the world, and those who would see you fail. You need to gird your loins for a battle.

Steven Pressfield writes about this in his book *The War of Art*.[1] He says, "The artist committing himself to his calling has volunteered for hell, whether he knows it or not. He will be dining for the duration on a diet of isolation, rejection, self-doubt, despair, ridicule, contempt, and humiliation."

He also says, "The sign of the amateur is over-glorification of and preoccupation with the mystery. The professional shuts up. She doesn't talk about it. She does her work."

While I truly don't think you have to suffer the "slings and arrows of outrageous fortune," I have seen many, many people fall prey to them.

One of the vital things *never* taught is *how to survive.* I mean literally to survive while you are on the road to becoming a self-sustaining professional. As I mentioned above, I've been talking about this very subject for years. I've done master classes at universities on this very subject, and to this day I've not found a single source that tackles this with any depth.

While I was performing in *The Phantom of The Opera* on Broadway I came to a realization. Artists, as a general rule, do not understand business principles and how they relate to their careers, and thus this book was born.

In the next few chapters I'm going to hit you with some truths and also lay a foundation so you have a place from which to start. Chances are, unless you've spent some time in the marketing world, you were never taught these concepts, and even if you were, you weren't taught how to implement them as an artist. Think of it this way: If you've never danced before, then you're not going to jump into an advanced ballet class. You need to understand the basics first and then grow into the more advanced classes. These chapters are fundamentals, the spark to ignite you into action. There is much more to learn, but if you haven't laid the groundwork you'll be building on a faulty foundation.

As you continue reading take those four steps I identified earlier and see how you can apply them to each chapter of the book and how you can apply them to your life.

YOUR DENTIST

Being a professional artists is one of the most difficult professions there is in which to make a living. There's no two ways about it. Everyone and their brother wants to be in a movie or a TV show. Everyone and their brother wants to be a pop star or movie star. If you asked your dentist if he wanted to be in a movie with Angelina Jolie, Tom Cruise or The Rock, chances are he'd say yes. But if you were asked to do a root canal…chances are you'd say no. Actually, unless you've got a medical degree in dentistry you couldn't do it even if you wanted to. That's one of the main differences between the arts and most other professions. *Anyone* can try their hand as an artist with no experience or previous skill required.

Here's another thing people don't think about: The entertainment field is the only profession where you can legally discriminate. It's true. If you don't fit the description, no matter what your skill level, chances are you're not getting the job. For performing artists this is a slippery slope because it can be used for good and bad. Creating equal opportunity for all races and genders is vital, but I've all too often seen the other side. Setting aside race, color, creed, or gender, the unspoken words you're "too big," "too short," "not pretty enough" become the daggers of what I call "the arbitrary." But these "rationales" rarely reach the artist's ear. For performers the phrases they often hear are "they went another way with the role" or "they didn't feel you were right for the role," and while those hold true in many cases, there are times when those words are covering other truths never shared outside of the audition room. The hard truth is that artists' careers are in the hands of the opinions of others. The same is true for a visual artist, graphic designer, fashion designer, on and on and on. You might be thinking, wait a second, I can see how this works in the performing arts but how can discrimination be so prevalent in the fine arts? Check this out:

I often talk about the arts in relation to a tennis match. When you watch Wimbledon or the US Open tennis finals, one person will win that title based *only* on their skill level that very day. It's how that person plays against the other person that will determine their success. It's not arbitrary. It's solely based on skill. Whoever is better that day wins, period.

I want you think about your favorite singer. Now think of your favorite song that singer sings. Can you hear the words in your head? I can guarantee you there is someone out there who doesn't like that song or any of that singer's other music.

But wait, you say: What about paintings or fashion design? I've been in auditions where two different actors were auditioning for the same role. Half of the room liked the first person and the other half of the room liked the second person, and these choices were not based on the auditioners skill alone, they were also based on the "opinion" each person in the room had about the person auditioning. This is the world of "the arbitrary." Some people love Picasso, some people don't get his art (and if you don't get it you need to look at his early work).

In the world of art, opinion plays a *huge* part in the success of the artist. Critics are a perfect example of this. Critics don't say, "In *my opinion* this piece of art is good or bad."

They say "This piece of art *is* good." or "This piece of art *is* bad." They determine *for you* what the result is.

I once had a conversation with a renowned theatre critic. He was a great and caring man who later became a dear and wonderful friend. I asked him this very question above. We were sitting together at dinner one night and had the following exchange:

Me: Why is it that in your reviews you say, "This show *is*" a certain way? Wouldn't it be more objective to state something like "In *my opinion* this show is this way?" and then let the audience decide what they feel once they've seen and experienced the show themselves?

Critic: James, we can't do that.

Me: Why not?

Critic: Because the audience is not smart enough to make up their own minds.

Those were the exact words that came out of his mouth! As my jaw dropped to the floor he simply smiled and said, "It's true."

Bottom line: You may love a piece of art, but someone else might hate it.

This phenomenon doesn't happen in professional sports. Sure, journalists may blame a team or a player for not playing well, but at the end of the day, the team or player with the most points usually wins and that is *always* based on the skill level brought to the table that day.

The trouble we face as artists is that once we begin to play the game in the pros everyone has a high level of skill just like professional athletes. But unlike pro athletes, as artists we are subject to opinion and critique based not only on our execution of that skill, but also how someone arbitrarily views that skill. It's similar to how a judge scores a gymnastics competition. It would be like a pro tennis player hitting a ball out of the court yet the line judge, because he "likes" the player or the player's execution, disregards the foul and gives the point to the player anyway. It's simply an unfair playing field.

You need to find something that will set you apart and put you in a position to mitigate the opinions, the naysayers, and obstacles—something that gives you the tools you need to play the game at its highest level.

Grab your Survival Guide notebook and write the last sentence you see below. You are going to come back to this later in the book and fill in the answers, but for now write it down so it's in your head as you proceed. And write it in the first person so it is actionable for *you*.

"These are the things I can do to level the playing field and give me the best chance of reaching my goals and dreams as an artist."

Starving Artist Syndrome

The idea of the "starving artist" is, in my opinion, a load of B.S. I've so often heard that struggling makes you stronger, that coal under pressure turns into diamonds. Here's some news for you: Coal under pressure does not turn into diamonds. It's simply not true. Diamonds are pure carbon, and although coal is made up of carbon, there are impurities within its structure that just make it chemically impossible to turn coal into diamonds. Sorry to break the news to you, but coal under pressure just gets you some crushed coal.

Sure, life lessons teach us many things, and we can use those as artists in our work. But what we need to understand is that an accountant or car salesman experiences loss the same way an actor does, a teacher experiences laughter the same way a singer does, and so on. What I'm saying is you don't have to starve to become a great artist. It's simply not true. And if you *were* starving you really couldn't do your job very well. If you did land a gig you'd be too hungry or sickly or tired to execute at your full potential.

Just like the misconception of coal and diamonds, you don't have to starve to become a great artist. You can simply *be* a diamond without all of that made-up pressure.

This is not to say you won't meet some pressures along the way, that's certainly clear, but what I want you to focus on are limiting those pressures so you have the best chance of surviving. As a young actor starting out in New York, I faced a boatload of challenges and had to navigate them all, which felt like juggling ten balls at the same time. So I'm going to share some realities below on what it takes to "make it" in New York without the sugar coating and rose-colored glasses so you can see those challenges up close and confront them. Dreams and passion are great and a vital part of achieving your goals, but the more prepared you are for the reality of what you're getting into…the more chance you'll have of succeeding. And the first step is identifying what you want to do, who you are, revitalizing your goals and dreams as an artist. This step starts with confronting the reality of your new chosen life…ALL of it.

In this chapter, I lay out some pretty eye-opening statistics. It shows you the pure, unbiased financial reality of living the life of a professional artist in New York City. I've done this because it is an essential part of surviving as an artist and it doesn't matter if you live in New York, Nebraska or the Netherlands. You *must* survive long enough to make a living wage at your craft, and you have to sustain that in order to truly survive and thrive. You need to confront the reality of this no matter where you choose to ply your trade.

If you can't eat, pay rent, clothe yourself, or travel to and from potential gigs, then you're not really playing the game and will have an even smaller chance at succeeding. And if you can't live, how can you ever pursue your dreams? You need money to do all of these things. Money creates stability, and from that stability you can create your future. So let's put the idea of the starving artist out of your head and focus on becoming *thriving* artists.

What you will see can be daunting. But remember that light burning inside of you, remember it and hold onto it.

You will need to confront the reality of what life as a thriving artist means. Looking at the harsh realities will allow you to understand, plan, and execute your path to reach your dreams.

Remember that thing people would say in high school? "I don't need algebra! I'll never use it in real life" or "Why do I need math?" I said it myself. I was like, heck, I don't need math to be an actor. Welcome to Artist's Math. You'll *need* it to survive.

There are many studies I can point to that break down income for artists, and no matter which of them you look at, the results are still the same: Most artists do not make enough money to survive. An article written in June 2019 shows that 90% of actors are out of work at any given time. For this illustration, I'm going to base the example below on something that is near and dear to me, the professional theatre (pre COVID-19 shutdown).

Actors Equity Association (AEA) is the Union that governs all professional stage actors (and stage managers) in the United States. There's also British Equity and Canadian Equity for those respective countries. For our purposes, we are focusing on the United States and I'm going to use the profession of stage actors, primarily because I've lived in this world my entire career. However, these same lessons apply to *any* career in the arts, whether that be singer, dancer, photographer, TV/film actor, fashion designer, and so on (for that matter, *any* career, even one not in the arts, can benefit from this information). But for now, let's agree we are looking at the life of an AEA member aspiring to make it on Broadway as an actor in New York City, again knowing that at the time of this writing, Broadway and all theatre has been completely shut down due to COVID-19.

The 2016 Theatrical Report[3] from Actors Equity Association included a pie chart for all working members of AEA and what they earned that season (p. 21). If you look at the pie chart it shows that 68% of all members of

Actors Equity Association earned $15,000 or less. That was before taxes. That covers nearly 70% of *all* working union members. The next higher bracket of earners is only 11% who earned $15–$25k, and then the next higher 10% earned $25–50k, again *before* taxes.

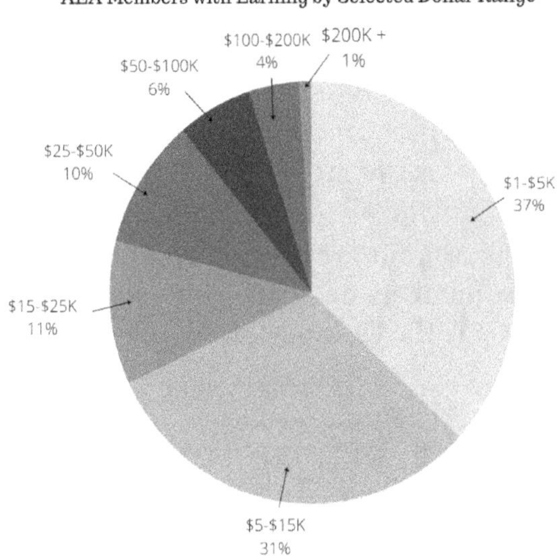

The above pie chart is taken directly from
the 2016-2017 AEA annual report.

This means 89% of *all* professional stage actors make $50k a year or less. I want to be clear here: It's not saying that all 89% make $50k a year. It's saying that the *top* folks (only 10% of *all* professional stage actors) earn $50k while the massive majority earn less than $15k per year, and this is all *before taxes*. This is *not* a living wage.

This reflects the "best of the best" in terms of stage actors. The top 5% of all professional stage actors make between $100–$200k per year and only 1% make over $200k. These figures are for those who get paid a guaranteed minimum union wage and are working under union guidelines nego-tiated by the stage actors union. This does not include nonunion actors who are often paid less and have even less stability in their workplace because there are no union rules to which the producers of the show must adhere. Additionally, given the incredible volatility of being an actor (i.e. your show could close at any time, the show has a limited run of only six weeks, COVID-19, you name it), there is absolutely no stability whatsoever.

But let's give you the benefit of the doubt. Say you're one of the top 10% of AEA members who make $50k a year. According to SmartAsset.com (an easy way to calculate your taxes), your yearly take home on $50,000 a year would be approximately $36,688.

Now let's look at your expenses living in New York City. I've based these numbers on apartment rentals as of April 2020 once the COVID-19 pandemic hit. I'm doing this for a few reasons.

It's the reality of renting in New York right now that rental rates are actually lower than before COVID-19, but also realize that *all* work for performing artists has stopped. There is no income expectation for the duration of unemployment or, at the time of this writing, any sort of subsidy directly for arts workers. Some have been able to rely on residual income from television and film appearances, but those who can maintain and sustain themselves on those residuals alone are very few. In short, I'm showing you rental numbers at the *lower* end of the spectrum.

According to rentjungle.com: As of April 2020, average apartment rent within 10 miles of New York, NY is $3,450 per month. One-bedroom apartments in New York rent for $2,940 a month on average and two-bedroom apartments rent for an average $3,662. Let's look at the numbers in greater detail. Grab your notebook and follow along. Artist Math starts here:

If you share a two-bedroom apartment in Manhattan, that's $1,831 per month (per person) times twelve months, which adds up to $21,972 for the year just in rent! This doesn't include utilities, food, clothing, transportation, classes, and all the other things you need. Now let's take your yearly post-taxes income of $36,688 and subtract your yearly rent of $21,972.

You're left with $14,716.

Okay, you might say "Hey, I've got almost $15,000 left over after I pay my rent! Not so bad!." Well, let's look at your other expenses and see how far this $15k goes.

Average cost of utilities and internet is about $178 per month. Split that with your roommate and you owe $89.00 per month, which is $1,068 per year.

Average mobile phone (on the low end) is about $50 per month times twelve months is $600 per year. You're looking at $1,668 for the year just in utilities and mobile phone expenses.

Subtracting this from your balance and now you're down to $13,048. This is what you have left to pay for food, clothing, classes, coaching, work materials, emergencies, etc.

Let's add those in because we're getting down to brass tacks here. The only way to actually have control over a situation is to confront it fully.

Monthly food expenses in New York City would be around $400-$500 a month so let's split the difference and call it $450.

If you take a class, and you *should* because you're competing with the best in the world, so a private voice coach will run you a minimum of $100 per hour (once a week) which is $400 a month, and that's on the low end.

Acting classes, again depending on the class, you're looking at between $300 (low end) to $500 a month depending on the class. So let's say $400 a month for acting class.

Dance class averages about $17–$20 a class and if you're a serious dancer (as was my wife who danced with American Ballet Theatre under the direction of Mikail Baryshnikov and later in five Broadway shows) you're taking class every day so that's about $400 minimum per month. For you non-dancers or non-singers out there, you can take those out of the mix, but I have to say that a triple threat is a triple threat.

Adding this up we are at another $1,650 a month just for classes and groceries.

Ok, now what about transportation? Forget the car situation. Parking in NYC is pure hell and the cost of parking in a garage is insane: Upwards of $500–$650 per month. Alternate side of the street parking is enforced in NYC, which means you have to make sure your car is parked on the correct side of the street or it will be ticketed or worse, towed. If you live in any city outside New York, Chicago, and possibly San Francisco, you'll likely need a car, especially in Los Angeles, so if this applies to you then you need to add car payment, insurance, gas, upkeep, and so on into the mix.

Public transportation in NYC is the way to go. You've got the subway or the bus. Both use Metro Cards, which is a card you swipe at terminals to gain entry to the transportation system. At the time of this writing a monthly unlimited card is $127, which allows you to ride as often as you want for that month.

I'm not even going to put in cab or Uber/Lyft options because at $50k a year with the expenses listed above, you shouldn't be taking cabs.

A little side note: A friend of mine once said the beauty of living *in* New York City is that if you don't have any money, you can always walk home. True, which includes in the *rain*, in the *snow*, and in the *freezing cold*. But yes, you can always walk home, and I've done it in all of those conditions.

Okay, this puts us at $1,777 a month for the above expenditures which is $21,324 per year. But we haven't discussed health and renters insurance, medical/dental expenditures, and all that good stuff. If you're covered under The Actors Equity Health Plan, you pay $100 per quarter (which is

$400 per year) *but* you have to have enough weeks of work to qualify for the insurance. If you don't qualify, then you can buy the insurance from the AEA provider for about $878 per month for one person. I'm going to go with the AEA Health Plan but the majority of actors coming into the city have not qualified for insurance with number of weeks worked. You can find less expensive insurance if need be. According to the website healthmarkets.com, the average cost of Insurance in New York State is about $610 per month. It's just the raw facts.

So adding the $400 for insurance into our total we now have $21,724 in basic essentials for the year which when subtracted from our remaining income of $13,048 leaves us with ***$-8,676.*** Do you see that? ***You're spending more than you make. .***

Take a breath. For experiment sake lets remove the acting, singing and dance classes from our yearly expenses. Without the classes your food, insurance and transport costs would be $7324 per year. Subtract that from the $13,048 and we get $5724. "Whew! I have some money left over! And it's almost $6,000! Great! But we haven't touched on any material goods like paper, envelopes, stamps, pictures, resumés, music that you buy, dance clothes, audition clothes, the gym, and on goes the list. Nor have we included any form of entertainment or leisure such as going to a movie or going out to eat with friends, nor have we touched on emergencies.

Oh, and guess what? We left out agent commissions! That's 10% off the top *before* you even get your check. So that's another $5,000.00 deducted from your total $50k (but yes, you still have to pay taxes on the entire $50k) *and* you owe 2.25% per week to the union which is a $1,125.00 addition to your yearly union dues, which are $118.00. Even after cutting out the yearly class expenses you're now left with ***$-519.***

"I'll be frugal!" you say. "I'll make more cuts. I won't eat as much food. I won't turn on the heat in the winter. I'll cut down my electrical usage. I won't go out or see movies. Okay, maybe one or two. I won't eat out or have drinks with my friends because I am dedicated to achieving my goals." Wonderful idea. One side note, I don't drink alcohol and never really have. I do know the cost of going out for drinks is *crazy*.

But heck…you had a great year artistically and you almost broke even. Compared to the vast majority of actors in the world you've had a stellar year. You're in the top percentile of income earners as a professional stage actor and you are really focused on success! You're ready to take the industry by storm!

You borrow some money from your parents to stay afloat and you start to audition, but the next audition doesn't pan out. That's okay, there's another one and another and another, but none of them work out. But hey! On your fourth audition you land a role in a thirteen-week run of an Off-Broadway show at a prestigious theatre. "Guess what Mom? It pays $615 per week for thirteen weeks! Woo-hoo!" You're making $7,995 before commission and taxes and everything else. By the way, I haven't even touched on the costs of paying student loans, amassed credit card debt or emergencies. Do you see where this is leading?

Your new weekly salary of $615 is not going to sustain you.

You *need* money and you need to find ways of creating it that will still allow you the freedom to pursue your goals. Make no mistake, the effort is still up to you and there are no guarantees made from the lessons I'm sharing. I am trying to open your eyes to the reality of life as an artist and also let you know that it *is* possible to achieve your dreams. You *can* do it. You just need to be prepared.

THE GLASS HALF FULL

You might be thinking, "Crap, what do I do now?" That's a pretty bleak picture of things. You might be living this reality right now and are uncertain how to get out of it. You might also be one of those people in the top five percent of income earners but have no certainty of what's coming next in terms of work.

This information is not bleak, it's reality and the only way to gain control of this reality is to confront it head on. If you hide from it or push it under the rug you will *never* be in control of your life. Instead, you will actually be at the mercy of everything around you, meaning the outside world forcing you to live a certain way rather than you living your life how you wish it to be. The world should be conforming around you and your goals, not the other way around.

I know we can't control the rain and the snow, but we can control your personal choices. An example of this would be someone telling you that you don't have what it takes to succeed in the field you've chosen. That you'll fail, that it's too hard, blah blah blah blah blah…

How many people listen blindly to the words of others? They listen even if those people have absolutely *no* knowledge about the very thing of which they're speaking. They certainly don't know you as well as *you* know you. It's that old saying: If someone tells you to jump in a lake would you do it? Those who are listening to the whims and negative thoughts of others are doing so to the detriment of their own lives. They are not confronting and controlling their own destiny, and they will forever wonder why they never lived the life they always dreamed of living.

Most of the people who are telling you "No," the naysayers, the haters—most of them tried and failed to achieve the very thing you are attempting to do. They are, in fact, trying to sabotage you. "What?" You say. "No they're not. They're just looking out for me. They don't want me to get hurt when/if I fail." Well, let's look at it this way. Those who have tried and failed to achieve the same goals you've set forth and are the naysayers in your life see your success as a slap in the face of their failure. Subconsciously, or even consciously, they are trying to stop you from achieving what they themselves could not. Stopping you makes them feel better about their own failure. If you succeed, to them it drives an emotional dagger into their own lack of success, in essence saying, "Joe did it. I didn't do it...I'm a failure." Those who are truly concerned for you, who care for you and love you, will support you and your efforts, especially if they understand how much those efforts mean to you.

Also be wary of "constructive criticism." We've all encountered it in one form or another. It's important to distinguish the form in which it comes. True constructive input would come in the form of "Today people are using this type of camera to shoot film," or "From my experience as a casting director your headshot should look something like this..." Good constructive input doesn't make you feel like an idiot or put you down.

You will also encounter those who gossip, those who tell you you'll have no chance, it's too hard, you'll starve, etc. You'll hear things like, "Wow, your paintings are so unique it might be hard for the average person to see the value, but I certainly like them" or "You were so brave for singing that difficult song. You did pretty well, considering..." You walk away thinking to yourself, "Considering what, exactly?" These are the people you should be wary of in your profession and in your life. These are the people who, after speaking with them, you just feel a bit "off." The underhanded complements, the talking about someone else when they're not there. Here's an insight: If someone is talking to you about someone else behind their back, then what are they saying about you to others when you're not there?

I told you the earlier lessons would be resurfacing later in the book, and here we are. Pull out your Survival Guide notebook and list out some people in your life who fall into the categories above. If you don't want to write them down, then make a mental note.

I know this is a hard thing to confront, but it's important.

Take a close look at the people around you. Really look at them and hear what they have to say. If they aren't supporting you, then you can confront them, nicely, and say something like, "I appreciate your words, but I'm really focused on achieving this goal. It's a dream of mine and it means a great deal to me. As a friend I'd really like it if you could support me as I pursue this goal." Listen to how they respond to you. If you get anything less than "I get it. I was just trying to help. I hope you achieve your dream and if I can do anything to help please let me know" then I would seriously consider *not* having that person in your immediate circle, and I would definitely *not* go to them for advice. Does this make sense to you? You don't need negative people in your life. You have an absolute *right* to have the kind of life *you* want, to be happy, healthy, joyful, fulfilled—and you have the absolute right to remove anything or anyone who is trying to stop you from obtaining it. By the way, this includes social media as well. These are your accounts, your profiles, your feeds. If you don't want something or someone there…remove them. It's *your* life. Live it!

There will, of course, be people who have real knowledge to impart to you about your chosen field, especially if they work in or have worked in your field and have achieved a certain level of success. Would you listen to advice from your dentist on the most effective use of lighting for a photo shoot if he has never done one? Of course not. Heed advice that is practical and applicable. Take the knowledge you can use to grow in life and in your profession. Seek those giving you real advice and real tools. Look for mentors. They will share true life experiences with you as they pertain to their success and failures in the industry. And here's the kicker: Truly successful people, and I mean both personally and professionally, *want* to see *you* succeed, and more often than not they will help you as much as they can. I'm going to pound this idea into you: Mentors are important! If you study some of the most accomplished people in the world, you'll see that they've had and used mentors in their lives. Knowing how they attained their success will serve as a road map for yours.

Don't Let Your Day Job Become Your Life Job

Reality check: Remember the story I shared with you about when I worked at Hackers, Hitter and Hoops? As a manager, I was making an hourly rate that would "get me by" and I could have stayed there for a while getting comfortable. But I had to take a chance. I didn't want my day job to become my life job.

An actress I know in Los Angeles had a "day job" as a waitress/bartender (like many actors do) at a nice restaurant in Studio City. This kind of work pays the bills and allows what many feel is flexibility to pursue their real career goals, but it can also be limiting and here's why: This actress had worked at this particular restaurant for over a year. She was an exemplary employee and did more than was required of her in terms of work. She was always on time, never asked for time off in the year she was there, and so on. In short, she was the kind of person you would want working for you.

One day she got a call from her agent telling her she had a callback for a TV pilot. She had auditioned and was now moving on to the next step in the process, which was a producer's session. The issue for her was that the producer's session was during the day and also during the time when she was scheduled to work at the restaurant. So, like anyone would do in this situation, she tried to get another employee to cover her shift.

No one would bite. No one wanted to or could cover that time. She even offered to work doubles for other people because this was a very important callback for a great television pilot that could very well change her career and move her forward on the path to pursuing her dream. But no luck. She couldn't get anyone to cover for her so she went to the manager and explained her situation.

While the manager, himself an actor, felt for her and said he "understood her situation," he told her she needed to find someone to cover her shift and if she couldn't find someone she'd have to come in to work. She pleaded with him, explaining this was a major callback and she had never asked for a day off and had not taken a sick day during her year working at the restaurant, etc.

This all fell on deaf ears to the pesky manager. He just repeated that if she couldn't get someone to cover her shift then she'd have to work, and now that he knew she had an audition that day, if she called out "sick" she would be fired. Nice guy, huh? Welcome to the real world.

Obviously, this was a very hard spot for her to be in. She needed the job to pay her rent, bills, and to eat, but at the same time she wanted desperately to follow her dream. She was faced with a real dilemma. If she quit to pursue her dream what would happen if she didn't get the part? Living on your savings is not an ideal situation as we saw in the Artist's Math section above. Savings are just that…savings. If you don't have a job you'll have no money coming in, but you *will* always have money going out. Again, simple math says if you keep that pattern up long enough, there won't be *any* money left at all.

In Los Angeles, even with great experience, it's hard to get a solid and "flexible" paying gig like the one she had at the restaurant. Our actress could be facing serious financial uncertainty and blow through what little savings she had.

Many people would have quit and if they didn't get the acting gig would have tried to find another job. I understand this mentality, truly I do. You have to remember I started in New York with very little. I had to survive on my own. I had parents who supported my career path and would help me out a bit when I needed it, but there's a time when you have to cut that umbilical cord. I know many of you reading this may not have the luxury of supportive parents, and if they are supportive they very well might not have the financial means to help you. This is a vital point for you to understand. Read it, read it again, and then read it again:

YOU ARE RESPONSIBLE FOR YOU

So what happened to my actress friend? She chose to go to the callback and she got fired. The audition went well, and she made it through to the network only to lose the job to another actress. She eventually got another waitressing gig (yes, it was stressful financially). She was living on fumes for a long time, and that cut into her ability to go after gigs in a solid and secure way. But here's the silver lining: About nine or ten months later someone from that pilot audition room liked her enough to call her in on another project—a print ad for a magazine. She got that gig and then another, and eventually over time built a pretty great career as a print model. Note this: She would have never gotten that print job had she not taken the chance. Yes, it sucked that she got fired and it sucked that she even had to go through that in the first place. But the fire was burning inside of her and she made the choice she felt was best for her.

The moral of this story is this: No one else is there to hold your hand or pick you up when you fall. Why? Because everyone else is picking themselves up and trying to make it through their own lives. There is no safety net unless you create it for yourself.

Wouldn't it be great if you had that financial safety net so you could do whatever you wanted to do, pursue your dreams, and tell that restaurant manager to go to hell when he said he was going to fire you? Wouldn't it be great if you could create that extra income from something connected to your skill set?

There's a term for it. and it's called "drop dead money." There's another phrase that people use with an "f" word and a "you" before the "money," but drop dead money is the nicer way of putting it. What does this mean? It means that you don't have to take a job you don't want to take because you don't need the money. So many people do jobs just for the money and they hate what they're doing. With drop dead money you can tell the person making your job difficult to "drop dead" because you don't need their job or their money. It's freedom.

Mentors and Skill Sets

This is one of my favorite aspects of entrepreneurial life. And here I am again pounding it into your head! Find someone who has achieved that which you wish to achieve and do what they've done. Research them, dig into what they did to get to where they got. I've read countless writings on Elon Musk, Richard Branson, Steve Jobs, Warren Buffet, and so on. While not "artists" in the traditional sense, they are certainly at the top of their games. Here's a cool discovery: I found in my research that they think much like artists think. They create and make things that will change the world. They take extraordinary risks and apply business principles to those ideas so they don't sit idly by just waiting to be discovered. They create the momentum, the movement behind their ideas and put them into action, which in turn creates a product. In a sense, they created their successes from nothing. They took an idea and made it real.

What's the lesson? Find someone who is doing or has achieved the thing you want to achieve, study them, and apply the tools that have created success in the past. You can tweak them and mold them to your craft, and also make a detour here and there, but take the road *more* travelled to success. You've already chosen a difficult path in the arts, why make it harder for yourself?

Artists used to have mentors, they used to participate in apprenticeships under a skilled or master teacher, someone who was doing the very thing they wished to learn, and moreover doing it at a very high level.

An apprentice can be defined as "One who is learning by practical experience under skilled workers a trade, art, or calling."

You would learn your craft under the guiding eye of someone who has mastered it or at least is highly proficient in that skill. Over time the function of apprenticeship has sadly been pushed to the wayside. It's no longer readily available to us as artists, or for that matter in most professions or walks of life. Heck, it's even hard to find this in a family unit. It's a free-for-all, and that's a shame because it's a lost opportunity.

Finding someone who has become successful in your field and learning from them will give you a major advantage over those who don't have that same information. Not to mention you'll have the added benefit of making your journey that much faster, easier, and cost effective.

As I mentioned in the opening chapters, I never had a true mentor to guide me, to help me make choices or to advise me based on their own practical knowledge of my chosen field. And while I did have various professors or colleagues who would drop little gold nuggets here and there, I had to learn the hard way, by grinding my way through obstacles I hit along the path. I continue to do so to this very day.

I'm not lamenting this "lost opportunity" because our individual journeys should never be compared to someone else's, but it has given me a deep-seated drive to help those who are in the same situation I was all those years ago. I want to help you reach your goals and dreams. I want you to look at what you need to become successful in the arts and entertainment field, your business field, your workplace, your family—I mean really look at it.

In order to succeed you have to be at the top of your game and that means refining your abilities, whether that be acting, singing, dancing, photography, design, or whatever. You *must* have the skill set to compete with those who are striving to reach the same goals.

This is not to say that you won't continue to learn and hone your skills, of course you will. We never stop learning. But don't think that longevity will come without some basis of craftsmanship. You might be a one hit wonder, and for some of you that might be enough, but for those who want a long and lasting career in the arts, a one hit wonder is just that…one hit and then obscurity.

So let's remove this misconception from the table. EVERYONE you will be competing with in your industry has skill, talent and some sort of drive. If they didn't they wouldn't be playing the game at a high level. And make no mistake, this is a competition. I don't look at it as a me vs them scenario, but more of a 'what do you have in your arsenal that will make you stand out' and thus have the best chance at getting the job in front of you. You MUST come with your "A" game all the time because others will be coming with their "A" game.

I had a martial arts teacher once say; "Never be fooled. Always assume that your opponent knows more than you." What does this mean? He literally meant that if we got into a fight with a stranger, we never know what to expect on any given day. Even though we had a certain level of skill, the other person could very well know way more than us and quite literally kick the crap out of us.

I've fortunately never been in a situation where I had to test his theory in martial arts, but I have been in that scenario as an actor. I've been up against other performers who were more prepared, better suited for the role, and knew more than I did. I was outclassed that day and they won the "fight" by getting the job.

A number of years back I was auditioning for a new feature film called The Green Mile. You may remember it. The film was based on the Stephen King novel of the same name and starred Tom Hanks and Michael Clarke Duncan (for which Michael would later be nominated for an Academy Award).

The film was being cast by the legendary casting director Mali Finn who was responsible for casting some of the most successful films of all time. I was to read for a role in the film that day and had about five pages of sides (script). I was prepared, but in those days many acting coaches and teachers would say things like, "Make sure you hold the script because if you look like you have everything memorized the casting director will think you've locked in your choices and that your audition will be *the* final and definitive performance you would give." The theory was that by holding the script and only being "familiar" with the lines gave the illusion that you are open to direction. I thought this was odd, but hey, I was listening to "experts," so taking this advice I had become familiar with the script, but I didn't have the entire thing memorized verbatim.

On the day of my audition I was sitting in the casting office waiting for my turn to read. Within less than ten minutes I was called into the room to read and there sat Mali with a video camera over her right shoulder. It was just her and me. She had no script in her hands. I sat down in front of her and she asked if I was ready. I said yes.

Normally there was a "reader" in the room. Someone who would read the other lines and characters in the scene with you while the casting director watched. Mali was alone. When I asked who I would be reading with Mali answered; "Me."

Remember, this was a five-page scene and she had no script in her hands. I asked her if I should "slate" (which means saying your name to the camera) and she said not to worry about it.

I had the first line of the scene, so I began. As I began, script in hand, I soon realized the "advice" I had been given about holding my script was a load of crap. Mali had the entire scene memorized. In fact, she had every scene and every character's lines memorized for *every* role she was casting that day, and she was seeing *multiple* actors for many different roles all in the same day. It hit me like a ton of bricks. I was completely unprepared.

Even though I knew the sides very well, I was not in any way up to the level I should have been for this audition. I did not get the job. Now, I should preface this by saying I was reading for a role I was not right for. The role called for a shorter person and I'm almost six-feet-four, but in all honesty that didn't matter. I was unprepared for the audition. Mali did call me in for other projects later on, and for those I made sure the lesson learned that day on *The Green Mile* was taken to heart. I did my very best to *never* repeat that mistake ever again.

If you are not prepared to play your "A" game then you will have a hard time reaching your goal. You might make it eventually, but it's like waiting for your opponent to make a mistake so your "less-than-prepared" action can overtake their momentary lack of execution. Think of this from the perspective of a tennis match. If you are playing a five-time Wimbledon champion, unless you are as prepared and as skilled as they are, the only way you'll win is if they continually make mistakes during the match.

Who would you rather be—the person waiting in the wings for someone to trip up or the person who is at the top of their game making their life happen, creating the opportunities, and overwhelming the competition by your skill, determination, and work ethic?

I hope you've chosen to be the second type of person. If you haven't, then I would suggest you put this book down now and do something else with your life. You've read far enough to see the reality of life as a professional artist, and you may even be living that life right now. If you can't take the heat or are looking for a shortcut, then cut bait now and run. But if you're inspired, then the second part of this book is where you'll get some answers and tools to take you to the next level.

What really matters is how you apply your skills in life while trying to achieve your goals as an artist. Remember, everyone in your field vying for success at the highest level has mad, crazy skills. That's a given.

You've got the mindset, now it's time to take some action.

PART II

Marketing

ARTISTPRENEUR

Each of the following chapters could fill an entire book of its own. As we move forward, I'm giving you an overview of the possibilities, the tools, and examples of each. This is the nitty gritty. The earlier chapters were preparing you for the work that comes with the tools I'm laying out for you. Learn these. Pay attention. This is what will set you apart.

Defining things always makes them clearer, and these definitions will be useful as you move forward in your life as an artist.

Artist: 1. a person who practices any of the various creative arts, such as a sculptor, novelist, poet, or filmmaker. 2. a performer, such as a singer, actor, or dancer.

Business: A person's regular occupation, profession, or trade.

Entrepreneur: A person who organizes and operates a business or businesses, taking on greater than normal financial risks in order to do so.

Interesting, right? As a professional artist you are focused on your art as the main means of income for yourself. Business is defined as a regular occupation or trade, and an entrepreneur is one who operates a business, taking on greater than normal financial risk in order to do so.

Put all that together and you get the *Artistpreneur*. Pretty much sums up the professional artist if you ask me.

Why then, if artists are truly entrepreneurs, have we never been taught what it really takes to survive in a world revolving around business? The answer is simple: We live to create. We live to inspire and change and motivate with our art.

Now is the time to learn the tools of the entrepreneurs, the marketers, the brand masters, and learn how to implement those tools in an effective way.

I want you to make a promise to yourself. I want you to change the way you think of yourself and your art. I want you to stop thinking about yourself as only an artist. I want you think about yourself as an entrepreneur. Change your mindset and you'll change your life. While there is never any guarantee that you'll reach stardom, or reach the level of a Picasso, Donna Karan, or Gaga, one thing is for certain: You will never make it if you don't try.

Grab your notebook and write down the names of your artistic role models. Once you've done that, I want you to write down the name or names of those people who are not in the world of the arts but whom you admire and respect for what they've accomplished in life.

Place each name on the top of a separate column. Under each column I want you to write what you admire about them, their careers, how you view them, what they stand for. Do they endorse any products? Have they invented anything? Have they "broken any molds" or taken any risks? Look at their social media platforms and see the number of followers, look at what they post, how they post it. Videos? Still photos? Blogs? Do you see what's happening here? You are creating a checklist of things that others are doing and have done. These are some of the things that have allowed them to rise up to success, and then leverage that success in other ways.

Whether they know it or not, these are entrepreneurial traits. Study them as you would your lines, your paint, your photography. As an artist, you've already chosen a difficult path. You are a warrior, a risk taker, a craftsman, a rebel. You are truly the embodiment of the entrepreneurial spirit. You are an *Artistpreneur*.

Combining these two worlds will give you insights and leverage that, until now, has not been used by many in the field of the arts. It's your time. It's time to clear away any misconceptions and define who you are and how you'll achieve your goals.

CONFUSION

The definition of "Confusion" in most dictionaries is something like the following: 1. Uncertainty about what is happening, intended, or required. 2. A situation of panic or disorder. 3. A disorderly jumble.

Understanding things to the best of my ability helps me to better apply the principles of and around the things I'm reading or studying. Take a look one more time at the definitions above because confusion plays a big part in us getting "stuck" and not moving forward to fulfill our goals and dreams.

All the definitions above all can be applied to the topic of the success. The first one, however, is what I want to focus on because the other two fall under or are a product of the first. If you are confused about something, then you are uncertain, you lack certainty, and if you lack certainty you can never move forward with confidence.

Here's an example of what I mean:

I was recently at a coffee house getting some tea. As I watched the barista making drinks, I couldn't help but wonder how he actually got anything done. This guy was in utter confusion behind the bar. It could have been his first day on the job, but he didn't look nor act like a trainee. He knew what he was "supposed" to do but he was utterly confused about *how* to do it.

He had two paper cups in front of him, and one of those metal pitchers they use to steam milk was sitting between the two cups. He reached for one of the paper cups and put it under the steamer, then realized the pitcher was empty, so he put it back on the counter and picked up a metal spoon. He then stopped, looked at all the cups in front of him, and put the spoon back in the metal container from which he had removed it. Next, he reached for a wet rag to wipe off the steamer spout but stopped before he did that, put the rag down and picked up the pitcher again, only to find the pitcher was still empty. So what did he do next? Naturally, he put the pitcher down, picked up a paper cup, and started filling it with milk from another pitcher. Once that was done, he realized he already put a third pitcher under another steamer and had to take that one out to prepare the very first drink he was making prior to me watching this escapade. At this point, I was as confused as he was just trying to figure out what he was doing.

Here's the kicker: He poured lukewarm almond milk into the paper cup he had *just filled* with whole milk, thus overflowing that paper cup. He stared at the cup in complete disbelief as if thinking, "How did this happen?"

This is a state of extreme confusion. He didn't know what to do, when to do it, or even how to do it. In the end he realized he hadn't even read the order sticker affixed to the side of the cup and did so only after all of this chaos ensued, and found he was making the wrong drink all along.

His uncertainty led to complete disorder and the product he created was a disaster, not salable, and was a revenue loss for the store. Each cup and its contents had to be thrown away and the drinks had to be made again. I would venture to guess this was not the only time he made mistakes at his job. Think of the losses he created by his confusion—time, products, revenue, the time of the customers and those working at the coffee house. It made him look "stupid" because to an outside eye the process seemed very simple. In truth he wasn't stupid, but he was uncertain about what to do. He was in a state of confusion, and that confusion became a liability to others and to himself.

The lesson here is that you really can't get anything done when you're confused. If you're confused about your path as an artist, then you won't be making the right choices, and this will hinder you moving on your path to success, just like the barista who was uncertain of what to do next. That uncertainty stopped him from completing the task(s) at hand. He might eventually get something done but think about the wasted time and effort it took him to do all of that work with no result, and even if there was some sort of product it was most likely not of high quality.

So how do you choose the right path, the proper course of action when you're stuck in confusion? How can you stop the confusion, create stability, and remove doubt so you have a clear and direct path to your target? Clearing away the confusion is truly the first step in getting to where you want to go, and doing it is easier than you think. It comes down to one word: *Identify*.

Identify one thing within the chaos, just one—not five, not thirty, not 100—but *one* thing you feel is causing you to be confused and hold on to it. This one item becomes the stable thing from which you will now base all other actions. Look at it, really see it, and hold on to it. If the barista had simply held on to the first item he was originally working on, focused on that and completed it before moving onto the next drink, he would have never gotten into such a mess.

Hold on to the cup. From there, all other actions follow. Read the sticker on the side of the cup to see what the contents of the drink are that you're about to make. Then the other steps would follow from there. Pick out the kind of milk, pour the milk into a pitcher, set the pitcher under the steamer, and so on. You see how one thing follows after another in a logical order? It's truly a simple process, but one we often pass over in our lives and careers. *This* is the first step to unleashing your true power.

When looking at your own life for that thing to create stability, you may find more than one. In fact, you may find quite a few things. Some of those things may be small and simple or they might be larger and complex. As I mentioned above, to help the barista all it would take would be to give him simple instructions on one thing in the coffee-making process at a time. Simply say, "This is a cup." Give him the cup, let him hold it, see it, and know what its purpose is. From there you expand to saying, "The sticker on the side of the cup shows you what drink you're making."

This might seem overly simplistic, but the same process can be applied to any situation in which there is confusion. Take the example of someone who has never driven a car. Show them the car, have them touch it, examine it. Then one by one show them the other parts of the car. The door handle, the steering wheel, the gas pedal, the brake, each time explaining what each thing is and how it works.

By identifying one thing at a time, you remove the overwhelm. Breaking down the chaos into smaller parts allows you to control one thing at a time and handle the smaller pieces one by one. Once you've handled all of them you will see you've handled the "overwhelm."

You might be thinking, "This is all well and good, but my confusion doesn't come from tangible things. And how the hell can it help me make more money with my art?" Confusion comes from thoughts, people, questions, and fears. You can use this same process to handle any and all of these things in the same way. Identify one thing, one fear, one person, one question, and from there once you have that thing clearly identified you can now work toward clarification of the things surrounding it and connected to it.

Have you ever walked through a park when a burst of wind suddenly gusts out of nowhere, sending hundreds of Fall leaves swirling into the air around you? You're standing in a little tornado of leaves, unable to identify one single leaf because of the swirling vortex. That's what the chaos of life can be like, only it's not leaves, it's choices, and people, and relationships, and money. Well, if you reached out and grabbed one leaf, then another and another and placed each one in a bag, slowly the chaotic tornado of leaves would diminish. You would start to take control of the swirling things in your environment and in turn create stability.

Sure, it can be a slow process to grab all of those leaves, but the point is that you don't want to try to grab all of them at once. Take one thing, one leaf, and stabilize it. That's one less thing now preoccupying you, and as you continue to do this, your life will become less chaotic and less confusing.

How do you do this in your life or career when its sitting on unstable ground? It's easier than you think.

Grab your Artist's Survival Guide journal. These next steps are going to be the foundation for your goldmine.

Make a list of things you know. These would be skill sets you have from studying your chosen field. Examples would be, I'm a photographer and I know how to use a camera, lighting, and Photoshop. I'm a singer and I know the technique of singing, how to read music, play the piano, etc. Write down which of the skill sets you could start to teach to someone else. Now write the first step you are going to take toward making that thing you want a reality. This can change over time, all we are doing here is creating stability in what can be an unstable environment.

Continue to define these points and act on them.

Following these simple steps will go a long way to creating stability and allow you to free yourself from confusion. They can actually be applied to any aspect of your life. In this case, we are using them to create stability and a foundation for you as an artist. You are an artist. People want to hear, see, and listen to you. I dare say the world *needs* what you create. Art can change the world and it is YOU who are making that happen. Let's build a sustainable way to help you get that done.

The things you've listed can be put to use to generate income and opportunity for you even when you don't have a "paying gig" as an artist. You're going to use them to build a new platform to expand your art, to create mailbox money (passive income that regularly arrives in your mailbox), and even make money while you sleep.

Brand: You Are Your Product

When you walk into an Apple store or go to Apple's website you see all things Apple—products made by and sold by Apple. You have to think of yourself as Apple. You have to think of yourself as a product and seriously focus on selling your product. Actors, singers, dancers, photographers, composers…accountants, teachers, no matter what your profession, *you* are your product. Sure, the result of the work you do as an artist, the art, is also a product, but you *must* think in terms of selling *you*. Let's take a deeper look at this.

You might think that what you *do* is your product, such as my songs are my product or the characters I play are my product or the photographs I take are my product, and yes that's true (and we'll discuss that in a later chapter), but getting down to the basics, you need to realize something very important: *You* are the first product you need to focus on and begin to sell. The two concepts of *you* and *do* go hand-in-hand.

Take our Apple example and notice how they've branded themselves in two ways:

1. As a company.

2. As a maker of incredible products.

You need to look at yourself in much the same way. Brand yourself as the pinnacle in your industry and follow up by creating amazing products that support your reputation (brand) to build confidence in the marketplace. If you do this, then you and your products will continue to be viable well into the future.

Most people in the arts don't really think of themselves in this way. There are a few, and you can probably guess who: People such as Lady Gaga, The Rock, Madonna, Elvis, even Andy Warhol had a very specific brand (notice that 3 out of 5 of these people are musicians?). Actors are known for certain types of films or plays, but for the most part they've not created that personal "thing" that stands out and breaks them out of the norm. Most of the time actors are known by the types of roles they play such as action hero, dramatic actor, comic actor, etc. or their public actions and persona.

I can't tell you how many times I run into people saying, "I just want to create great art." Truth: If no one knows your art is there you'll be sharing it in a vacuum, which is not good for anyone but your own ego.

Apple is branding themselves in a specific way, so the consumer (audience) is excited to buy whatever it is they're selling. Same with Lady Gaga. Whether you like her music or not, she entices you through her branding to want the new and improved product (song/concert) each and every time she promotes it, just like Apple launching a new or updated iPhone, computer, or watch. You need to make yourself like Apple so that everyone in your industry thinks of *you* as the go-to person for whatever job they need.

Here's a real-world example: Let's say you are going to buy a new car. You've researched the car you want, know the numbers, have gone to every website there is to get as much data as possible, and with all of this ammunition in hand you head out to the car dealership.

If you've ever purchased a car from a dealership, then I'm sure you've had a multitude of varying experiences. I'm going to share one of mine, something personal that happened to me, which will illustrate that no matter your industry, *you are your brand.*

I was in a high-end car dealership buying a new car. The lease was up on my old vehicle and it was time to get a new one. When I walked in, I was greeted very nicely and was then turned over to a salesman. Although the salesman was a nice guy, I quickly discovered I knew more about the vehicle than he did (and he was a veteran salesperson at this dealership). In all honesty, this didn't bother me. I knew what I wanted, the guy was nice, and we made the deal. Here's where the story becomes relevant to personal branding.

After I made the deal, I was introduced to the "finance guy" who was going to set up the lease. He sat down and started saying "sign here, sign here, etc." He didn't say, "Hello, thank you for purchasing a car." Not even a handshake. This guy was immediately cavalier. He seemed like he didn't want to be there, was rude, was trying to be sarcastic, and told horrible jokes. In short, he was a jerk.

Both the salesman and sales manager, who were standing with me, had looks of shock on their faces. They tried to spin it as "that's how he always is" and laugh it off. This attitude lost them a sale that day. The finance guy's personal brand, how he represented himself and how he engaged with the customer (me) caused me to walk away.

The salesperson and I spent about forty-five minutes looking at vehicles, going over all of the various options they had in stock. We agreed on a specific vehicle and price, but it all came to a screeching halt when this finance guy with no sense of self-branding came into the picture.

The finance guy thought the deal was done. He didn't seem to care what image he put forth, thinking all that was needed were a few signatures. But the deal wasn't done. He didn't think he was selling himself (because the salesman had sold me the car) but he was sorely mistaken. Not only was he selling himself to me, but he was also selling the dealership. If the dealership hired this guy then they are acknowledging his actions that day reflect those of the dealership and are in line with how they treat customers.

The dealership knew this going in and did nothing to correct or handle the way the finance guy treated people. His personal brand was that of a jerk, and that was not in line with what I wanted to deal with, so I stood up before signing even the first paper, thanked the two men who helped me out that day, and walked out of the dealership.

Within minutes I was called by the sales manager who started apologizing profusely for his employee's behavior. I acknowledged the manager and was told this guy was one of three finance people and if I were to come back they would assign me to someone else.

Here's where the lack of personal branding negatively impacted the dealership. I did go back the next day and I was assigned to a different finance person, but because of the experience I had the day before, it put me in a position to bargain. You see, I could simply head to another dealership with the negotiated numbers in hand and make the same deal, and the original dealership knew it. To keep my business, they squeezed out commissions and gave me the car at an insider price.

I'll be totally honest. The little extra money I saved didn't matter to me. I had now spent two days dealing with the car situation when it should only have taken me one. The cost of my time versus the amount of money I saved is not equitable. I would have made more by working on various projects during that time than I saved on the car.

I'm using this example to illustrate how your personal brand is an asset but can also be a liability if you're not careful. On a personal note, I built my own brand to a great place, had an incredible career and trajectory, and then crashed it. Through various events in my life, I hit rock bottom and completely shattered my brand, and I mean *completely shattered*. I went from top to bottom overnight, and I was faced with some real challenges. I took responsibility and began again.

I had to learn how to rebuild from a place of inner truth, honesty, and integrity. I learned a great deal during that time, most of all how you must *live* the life that exemplifies that which you wish to attain. Merely speaking the words is not enough. Your actions are the key. They are the key to your integrity, your success, and ultimately your life. You must define who you are, what you stand for, and live it with integrity, for that is the only thing that will gain trust and sustain your brand.

How do you start this? You need to define who you are, what you represent, and how your personal brand works in relation to the project, film, play, gallery showing, portraits, or whatever you are working on, even in life. You are selling *yourself*, and you are a vital commodity.

What have I been telling you? *Artists are entrepreneurs.* By clearing away confusion and defining your brand, you are on your journey. Use this road map, this series of steps, to implement the exact same tools used by successful entrepreneurs and apply them to your life as an artist.

These tools are applicable to *you*. They can and will help you break out of the chains of the "starving artist" syndrome and into the life of a thriving artist.

The choice is yours.

The Power of a List

I have a dear friend who starred in a few shows in London's West End. She's very successful, but like everyone in the field, once her show closed she was relying on agents and casting directors for her next job. She's well known enough to start fielding offers, meaning different producers and directors know and respect her work and offer her jobs without having to always audition. But she was still at the whim of if and when they called.

On this particular occasion in question, she had wrapped up a show contract and was unemployed. I asked her what she had on the burners and she told me she was putting together a concert of some sort in the UK. This was of her own origination and she was creating it by herself…entrepreneurial. However, when I asked her how she was going to let people know about the concert she simply said, "Social media."

Me: "Is that it? Do you have a newsletter?"

Her: (Insert awesome British accent here) "A whaaat?"

Me: "A newsletter, something you can send out to your fan base by email."

Her: "Email? How would I do that?"

Me: "Do you have a list of your fan base from the show you just did? A list? Of email addresses? You can send a notice of the concert directly to your fan base via email."

Her: "I'm putting it out on social media darling, isn't that the same thing…sort of?"

While social media is super-important (and I will be covering that in a later chapter), it is not the same as a list of people dedicated to you, your art, your creations, all of whom have, through a series of steps, proven to be loyal and ardent followers.

Not only did my friend *not* have a list, but she didn't even know what it was in relation to marketing herself. Check this out: She was starring in a show on the West End for a couple of years. That theatre had over 1,600 seats and there were eight performances per week. 1,600 x 8 = 12,800 people. At least 12,800 people seeing the show (at full capacity) every week, and at least 665,600 people seeing her each year (12,800 x 52 weeks).

Imagine just for a second if my friend had a way to collect the names and email addresses of those who came to see her in the show? She's an amazingly talented performer, and I can guarantee most of the people who saw her perform in that show would go and see her in something else.

Here's a little online marketing statistic for you: Each email in a list is worth at least $10 in possible revenue. Actual studies show that with various tools in place you can actually get the value of an email address to over $19 per email. You can check this out at DBMarketing.com. So what does this really mean? Let's just take the $10 figure as our example.

My friend, had she created some sort of fan newsletter, conservatively could have captured 10% of her audience with a free newsletter offer allowing her fans to get updates on her upcoming projects. In one year, based on the number of seats above, that would have been 66,560 fan emails. Simple math tells us that if each email is statistically worth $10 then she has the possibility of creating an additional $665,600 in revenue each year. What?! Yep, it's true.

Let me break this down for you further because a list is a massively powerful tool: My friend could send out an announcement about her new concert in an 800-seat venue. Say she, conservatively, charged $45 per ticket—that's $36,000 gross revenue per night. That's only 800 people of her list of over 66,560.

Say she recorded a new CD and she sends an email out about it to her list. What if 20% of her list (13,330 people) buy her new CD at $9.99. That's $133,166.70 from *one* email. Do you see now the power of a list?

You might not be in a situation where you have the ability to capture an audience like she did, but the brilliant part is that it doesn't matter. You can still build an audience and an email list no matter where you are in your career. You build one step at a time, follow some simple rules, and your list will grow. Even if you had 100 people on your list and each of them bought something from you for $10 then you'd have an extra $1,000.00. As you grow and expand your list you grow your potential to generate income through that list. And you can use it in multiple ways with multiple products.

There are many software programs available to help with this. They are called "CRM" systems. CRM stands for *customer relationship management*. To put it simply, a CRM system allows you to manage business relationships and the information associated with them. Some are free to use up to a certain point while others have a monthly subscription fee. You may know some and might even use one. MailChimp and Constant Contact are two examples of platforms that have a free version. Once you hit a certain number of contacts on your list then they bump you up to a paid monthly or yearly service. Others like ActiveCampaign and InfusionSoft are higher-end platforms that have a free two-week trial period, but then go to a monthly or yearly subscription after that.

By using email lists you have an instant and direct way to communicate to your audience and fan base. Here's some other cool stuff: Through these CRM platforms you can actually see who on your list opened the emails, who clicked the links, who bought products, and who didn't do any of those things. Why is this important? Statistics! Customers (audience, fans) who have purchased something from you before are more likely to do so in the future. Using the statistical tools in the CRM allows you to see who those people are, which is vital information.

For example, when I produce my annual Holiday Concert, I send out a series of emails to my insiders access group, which is a specific segment of my audience base. These are people who have joined (subscribed to) my free newsletter and have continually supported my concerts, events, etc. With one simple click of a keyboard button I can instantly and directly communicate with my base. In the email is a link to purchase tickets to the concert and we even offer a VIP experience that always sells out within a couple of hours. What I am not doing is waiting for someone to hire me, discover me, search me out, or offer me a job...I'm taking control over my career and creating opportunity.

You can do the same thing with your art, photography, voice lessons, writing, painting, and on and on and on.

Again, I understand you might not be in a situation like my friend on the West End, or even me, in that she and I have had the blessings of being in some pretty big shows that had huge audiences. Make no mistake, those who reach a certain level and sustain it have worked their asses off to get there, but that does not mean that they have implemented any of these tools. And it also does not guarantee longevity or financial stability.

Read this and take it to heart: *It doesn't matter where you are in your career.* When you apply the business tactics of the entrepreneur you can *create* that audience where none before existed. This list will be the foundation for your future. It will be the income generator when you are between gigs. Had these tools been available to me when I started my career or had I learned them earlier, I can guarantee you I would have used them to build my brand. And to put it bluntly, if you had something like this in place and had started building it a year ago, then you wouldn't be worried about unemployment right now.

This is your goldmine. This is the power of a list.

Social Media

Everyone is on social media. It consumes our lives and, in my opinion, at times can become a detriment. That being said, it has opened up the world to communication from anyone, anywhere, at any time, about anything. We can share stories, thoughts, images, and videos across the planet in mere seconds. It is used to educate, to unite, and also to divide. It is a powerful tool and, when used correctly, can help you build your career.

Notice I said, "when used correctly." If you want to build your audience you need to utilize the steps above to implement this on social media. If you are an artist, I strongly advise you to separate your personal pages from your business pages. Facebook allows you to have a "fan" or "business" page as well as a personal page, and you should absolutely keep them separate.

Remember, you are a brand and your posts should reflect this. If you start doing a little research you'll see that some of the top artists in the world don't have web pages. They use social media as their web page. In fact, one prominent actress I know has a webpage, but when you go there it just links to her social media accounts.

There are different reasons for the use of social media and webpages, and each has its own purpose. Ranking in Google searches is one. When you are building your brand, you need to outflow as much as possible. Having your name and website pop up on Google before anyone else is important. According to Leverage Marketing, the average person won't go past the first five results on a Google search. That means they don't even leave the first page. You need to make sure you are on that first page when they search. People need to know and be able to find your name so they can enjoy and buy your art. If no one knows you're there then how will they know what you're selling?

Example: If a guy opens a doughnut store, puts that store on an obscure corner in some town but does no advertising, he won't have much traffic and won't sell his product. Why? Because no one knows he's there. But if he builds his store on a prominent street where tons of people pass every day, and in addition he also advertises to a specific target audience, his chances of making sales rises dramatically.

Do you think this doughnut store owner is going to be sharing posts and advertising how cute his dog is in every post? Or posting a photo of himself standing in front of a fancy car? He might if the dog is eating one of his doughnuts or if the car is made out of his confectionary creations, but if the posts don't somehow connect back to him selling doughnuts, he wouldn't do it. You see this every day. You get emails everyday about some special or some product—you're on someone's list yourself. You need to think of your brand on social media the same way. What message are you conveying? Remember, you are an *Artistpreneur* and you must keep this in mind when you're posting.

Grab your Artist's Survival Guide notebook and take some notes.

Find some of the top artists you like and admire. Study what they are doing on social media. The Rock is killing it. He's personable, and yet at the same time most of his posts have something to do with his businesses. It's also interesting to look at the ratio of his posts. Look at the number of posts in which he talks about his film and TV projects compared to his posts about the products he's creating or with which he has endorsements deals. It's pretty heavy on the product side.

Also realize that each social media platform is different. Different formats, different audiences, and different longevity. Take YouTube versus an Instagram Story, for example. IG Stories are gone in twenty-four hours, whereas a YouTube video is always there. You need to look at the differences in each platform as you would the differences in media outlets. TV versus film versus print versus live. The content you create for each platform will be different.

All of this is to say you need to have a consistent message to share with your base. It can and probably will change over time, but by creating consistency you'll start to build a loyal following. People will want to connect with you because of your message and your story. Your audience will grow, and these are the people who will be interested in what you are doing and what you have to offer.

Here's the other power of social media in the entertainment industry: Believe it or not, studios look at the size and influence of an actor's social media presence during casting. Yep, it's true. If one actress has 8,000 followers and another has 800,000, you can bet your butt they are going to lean toward the actress with the larger following. It means she's active and there are people who engage with her accounts. Engagement on social media platforms means people will be more likely to watch the things she's doing and in relation to a film that means more likely to buy a ticket.

So grab your notebook and check out the social media accounts of some prominent people in your chosen field. Look at what they post and how they post. You'll start to see some patterns. Write down what you can do on your social media platforms to start getting your brand awareness out to the public.

The key is to keep your brand and message consistent.

INFLUENCE

Why are celebrities used in commercials and advertisements? Why are they paraded out and asked their opinions on politics and social issues? One simple word says it all: *Influence.*

Influence impacts the world in massive ways. Who we listen to, what we watch, the clothes we buy, the food we eat, the diet, the car, the watch, the handbag, how we vote, and on and on and on. I'm not going to go into the right or wrong of these things because everyone has their own opinion, but what I will say is that we are swayed by the influence of others. When your favorite celebrity or sports figure endorses something, it carries weight. It's why companies pay these people huge amounts of money to appear in their commercial to wear their clothing, drink their drink or drive their car. Their influence is valuable, *very* valuable.

When we think of a brand and the message behind the brand, we can see how this is reflected in our everyday life. Matthew McConaughey doing the Lincoln commercials, The Rock branding Under Armour, Charlize Theron with Dior. Their personal brands match the product and thus the products matches the brand. These celebrities bring massive value to the products and the companies. By having them wear, represent, and talk about their product, it increases the chances *you* will buy it. If it's cool for Matthew McConaughey to drive a Lincoln, then heck, I'll be cool for driving one too.

You get how this works, right? This is the power of influence, and it is incredibly valuable not just when it comes to endorsements, but also when it comes to building your career. Create a good and honest personal brand and doors will begin to open. Tarnish that brand and the doors will close. Right or wrong, your brand affects the influence you have and the impact you have on the world.

I talked about the power of social media in the previous chapter and how studios are looking at actors' social media reach as part of the casting process. The more followers you have the more people will be likely to tune in to your next gig or buy your next painting. Influence is vital, and you can use it to build your career and create independence from the "old school" way of getting a job. This is why your brand is so important. You want to build a trustworthy brand that is respected and valued. Trust me on this. I've lived it. As I mentioned earlier, I had a brand that was flourishing. I was well on my way to some great things, and then I crashed my brand and nearly burned it to the ground.

I became, to some, unsalable. All the work I had done in my life and career seemed, in one brief moment, to go up in smoke. I was forevermore marked with a "scarlet letter" of sorts. But for me, I wasn't going to just succumb, so I began to rebuild. I took responsibility. Much work needed to be done, and I still work on it to this very day. I never point to anyone but myself for all that has happened in my life. Reality versus perception. I looked at it (and still look at it) as my responsibility, both the good and the bad. You can't go back in time, you can only move forward. Create anew. By taking responsibility for your life, *all* of your life, you can be the one to build it, to change it, to create it, or recreate it.

I share this with you only to say, wake up! Look at your life, your choices, those around you, those with whom you align yourself, the things you write about on social media. If you are willing to own them, be them, take responsibility for them, live with them *forever* then this is your brand because they will *never* go away. They will affect the circle of influence you have now and in the future. But if you know and understand this, then you can use this influence to build your artistic dreams into something unstoppable. You can use your influence to change the world with your art. You won't need to rely on others to get you a job—you can create your own path.

I hope you see how this works. With influence you will be asked to do things without having to audition, pitch, sell, hope, or wait for a call. It's called *leverage*, and it's vital in growth.

Let's look at how leverage works.

Leverage can be defined as to "use (something) to maximum advantage."

Pretty simple really.

Let's say you have the only tire repair store within fifty miles of your town. John blows a tire on his car and needs it repaired. John's choices are to take his car to you or get it towed to another store fifty miles away. More likely than not he's going to take his car to you. You have leverage. How you use that leverage is the key question. Are you exchanging properly? By this I mean are you going to take advantage of John and overcharge for the tire because you know you can or are you going to give him a fair price so you build his trust for the future? I've known people to do both, and both have varying consequences. How are you going to use it? This is where your brand comes into play, and how you want to represent your brand to the public. It also might depend on the circumstance of the deal and the parameters and details at play. Remember my story of the car salesman? Leverage. Know this: The more leverage you have the greater your chances of getting what you want.

This is not a bad thing, this is just reality. Building your brand as an independent entity will give you incredible advantages as an artist. It's what makes household names, and it's what sets them apart from the crowd. Obviously, not everyone will become a superstar, but you can indeed create a brand that will have influence and leverage in your field. I know plenty of people who are Broadway stars and are super well-known by that circle, but to the general public their names would mean nothing. That doesn't mean they don't have leverage. They have leverage on Broadway. They could also leverage their Broadway fame to create fame in another field where they are unknown. Leverage. When you create leverage more doors will open for you, which means more opportunity, which means more freedom.

Think on this. Study it and implement a daily practice of building your brand to have influence so you can leverage that influence to get your art out into the world.

Like anything, it takes consistency and commitment. By building influence you are taking another step to control your life and your career.

One last point on branding: Your brand should be part of *you*, meaning it should be truthful to your core values and beliefs. If someone meets you "off the record," then you should be a representation of that brand no matter where you go. I'm sure you've heard the terms "on" and "off," as in "He's always *on*," or "He only *turns it on* when he's in the public eye." It's often used in a sort of derogatory way for people who are never themselves because they're always putting on airs or putting up a façade for the public. And while it is true that celebrities may act differently when they're on a red carpet compared to when they're sitting at home in front of the TV, you must also realize that your brand will indeed permeate your personal life. Build your brand on the truth of who you are. It's sustainable that way, and it's truthful.

What Do I Sell?

Okay, so you have a personal brand and understand the impact your brand has on social media and indeed anything you do in the public eye. You also have a list and understand the power of influence and leverage. But, you may be saying, "I still don't have a job and I need to make money!"

Now what?

Now you put these tools to work. By implementing them you can put together a formidable foundation that will not blow over in the wind and will help you survive during the lean times, during the down times, during the in-between-gig times. Like what you ask?

You can create an online course teaching voice, dance, art, photography, filmmaking, or whatever you're into. Create an online gallery where you can sell your photographs to your list. You can write a book about something unique and publish it on Amazon. These are just simple examples of things you can do.

Grant Cardone wrote a book called *The Millionaire Booklet*[2] and this little booklet changed how I saw business. On page 21 he breaks down a few ways to make a million dollars. He literally reverse engineers the math of making $1 million bucks. Here are a couple of my favorites:

5,000 people pay you $17 a month for 12 months

2,000 people pay you $42 per month for 12 months

2,000 people buy a $200 product

Do you see now how the power of a list makes sense? You can create a membership site (yes, it's done all the time) where people come to your site for a monthly fee. In exchange you give them content, video content, written content, blogs, recipes, lessons, whatever makes sense for you. The numbers above are just examples. It's simple math. You can tweak it however you want. But when you break it down in this way, it doesn't seem insurmountable, right?

Just play with the numbers (Artist's Math):

1,000 people pay $17 a month for 12 months = $204,000

That's still not a bad addition to your yearly income. And if you're in that high percentile of stage actors who make $50k per year, that $204,000 is more than quadruple your yearly take-home pay.

Grant Cardone's Millionaire Booklet inspired me to see things in a different light. Many, many people are doing this *very* successfully. It's not that hard. It takes understanding and work to implement the tools, but you can do it. Others are doing it, so why not you?

Here's the other number equation that relates to this book. And if we take our actor from above making $50k per year (before taxes) we see this:

Salary $50k x 20 years = $1 million

This means that if you make $50k net take home (after taxes) and didn't spend any of it, in twenty years you would have a million dollars. So why not create something that makes you residual income or mailbox money? Create a program you sell for a monthly fee and you can indeed create stability.

Here's the amazing part: You can create these online programs *while* you are still pursuing your career as an artist. It's not an either/or thing. There are multiple ways to use these tools so start thinking of ways you can expand. I'll give you a couple examples right here:

You can create a membership site where you charge a monthly fee and in exchange your fan base or customer base gets a specific program. That program can include exclusive weekly live group coaching calls, a private Facebook group for all members to interact, or exclusive content to help them or teach them.

Here's a real-world example: I have a photographer friend who loves photography and creating photographs. He also teaches people how to take photographs. He does this both in person at small events traveling around the world, and he also has an entire program dedicated specifically and only to Leica Camera presets. He sells those courses online and makes a *ton* of money all while he's still doing what he loves most—taking photographs. He's an artist of the highest caliber and is using these tools to expand his brand. You can do the same. It's only limited by your imagination, your desire, and your commitment to put in the work.

Do What Others Won't

When you enter into a competitive world such as the arts where everyone is vying for a very limited number of spots on the roster, you need to think in terms of what will set you apart from the masses. You need to think about doing things others won't do.

This can come in many different forms from your work ethic, to your outflow, to how you brand yourself and what you do. Something as simple as getting up earlier than everyone else and "having at it," thus beating them to the punch, can work wonders.

Again, I'll take some examples from my own life as an actor. I realized very early on that in order to have any chance at success in this industry, I had to go the extra mile (and get this…other people had that thought as well). One of the things I did was to take care of my body. Why would this be important you ask? I'm not just talking about eating well and going to the gym, I'm talking about getting enough sleep and not being seduced by the "Bright Lights Big City" allure.

Okay, what do I really mean? There's a great story about the producer Jefferey Katzenberg: I read how Jeffery woke up every morning at 5:00 am (LA time) to begin his day. This included working out and being able to get on calls, eating, etc. So when I heard this story and looked at Jeffery's success,

I made a correlation. I certainly wasn't at his level of success, nor am I at this moment, but I took away something very valuable from his story: I saw young artists, actors, musicians and so on all playing the Hollywood game or the Big City game—going out, partying, trying to network into the wee hours of the morning. That's all well and good, but then I would also see those same actors the next morning bleary-eyed and sometimes hungover at the very same audition I was attending. I'm not saying they weren't talented, but there's no way anyone could tell me they were at their "peak" during that audition.

Networking and creating contacts is a vital part of any business, but you must absolutely be prepared when any opportunity comes your way, and that preparation starts with *you*. Take care of your body. I don't drink, I don't smoke, have never used drugs, and eat as best as I possibly can. I also try and get a minimum of seven hours of sleep if at all possible.

Here's the thing about sleep and peak performance: Some people burn the midnight oil and work until all hours of the night. That's okay once in a while for a deadline and such. But doing that on a regular basis is detrimental. Trust me when I say that if you are well rested and have enough sleep, you'll accomplish way more in a shorter amount of time than if you're exhausted and in a fog. Sleep is important.

So do what others won't. Look at what others in your field are doing and then figure out things you can do that the competition is not doing. What kind of marketing can you do? Remember, *you* are your product.

Here is something else that I did while I was on tour with *The Secret Garden* musical. I knew most casting directors didn't take kindly to people showing up and knocking on their doors. Dropping off a picture and resume was okay, but I wanted to make sure that while I was on tour for a year-and-a-half that I wasn't "out of sight out of mind" to the casting agents. What I did was this: Each city we performed in was kind of unique. Los Angeles, Chicago, San Francisco, St. Louis, and so on. I got post cards while we were sitting down in each city and I would send off a little "Hello from San Fran" or a "Greetings from Chicago" to casting directors back in New York. I thought this was a cool and unique way to keep my name in front of them. I would write briefly about the show and send warm wishes. The casting directors were getting something a little different. It wasn't an "in your face" kind of communication, but a cool postcard from cities around the country.

I had no idea if it was making any difference until a New York casting director (one of *the* biggest theatrical casting directors at the time) happened to come to the show while we were in Toronto. He was in Canada because he had cast another Broadway show that was about to open its tour in Toronto and stopped by to see our show while he was in town. Everyone in the cast knew he was in attendance and he came backstage afterwards to see a few of the principle actors. As he passed me in the hall he said, "Great job, James," and he continued down the hall to one of the dressing rooms when he suddenly stopped, turned to me and said, "And oh! I *love* your postcards! Keep sending them!" He smiled and walked right on into the dressing room of one of our leads. That's how I knew my idea had worked. This man later went on to cast me in a few big shows. I still had to bring the goods at the auditions, but those postcards gave me a little edge over others who were not promoting themselves in a similar way. Most of all it came from a good place. I really loved sending out those cards, and to this day I still send holiday gifts to different casting and production offices I've worked with over the years.

Here's another real world example: When I first got to New York City, I would pound the pavement for acting jobs. I grabbed Backstage Newspaper and would, like every other actor of the time, scour the paper for auditions. There are hundreds, even thousands of wannabe actors in NYC, and obviously the competition was and is fierce. All of us were constantly vying for only a few jobs. I was not in the union at the time, so there were limits on the access to the big jobs, the better paying jobs. However, each union show was required to hold open calls and as I mentioned, anyone and everyone wanted to audition for them, but there were only a very limited number of slots available.

The story I'm going to share with you was repeated day after day for months until I got my break. In order to get a slot for an open call, you had to sign up on a list, and once that list was full then there were no more slots available. Needless to say, not everyone would be seen who wanted to be seen. This audition was being held at the Actors Equity Building, and the doors to the AEA audition space didn't open until 9:00 am. On days like this I would get up at 6:00 am, shower, eat, and prep my audition materials. I would head to the AEA building and by 7:00 am (in the dead of winter) I was standing in a line with about seventy-five other people in front of me waiting for the doors to open. I wanted to guarantee myself a slot, so I got there early, and yet at 7:00 am there were already 74 people ahead of me. By 9:00 am there were already 150 in the line. I wanted to guarantee myself a slot, so I got there early, and yet at 7:00 am there were already 74 people ahead of me.

Here's a side note: It was at one of my first open calls that I met the casting director from the postcard story above.

I will tell you this: During those days standing in line, countless people gave up. They would see the length of the line, feel the twenty-eight-degree weather, and simply give up and walk away. They had taken themselves out of the game before even setting foot on the field. But many of those who stayed built long-lasting friendships with each other. Most of them, if they had the skill set, had some success. Some went on to star in shows, get Tony nominations, Tony awards, and some even became movie and TV stars. To this day a few of those people are still in the game, we are all still friends, and although we've attained different and varied levels of success, we all remember and reflect on those times standing in the cold for days on end.

My persistence eventually paid off. Because I put in the effort, put in the work and was willing to push myself out of my comfort zone, I eventually got my "big break." I booked the national tour of the Broadway show *The Secret Garden* from an open call. I would go on to understudy one of the leads, which then led me to *Cyrano,* my first Broadway show, which then led me to a starring role in the Off Broadway production of *Milk and Honey,* which then led me to my first starring role on Broadway in the Lincoln Center revival of *Carousel.* All of this happened within three years, and it didn't happen by sitting on my hands and waiting.

If you want to survive long enough to make your dreams a reality, then you must think outside the box. What I shared with you above is a given. Anyone who wants to have a career as a professional artist must have that kind of dedication. I want you to think about what you can do when you don't have a gig, or when you're not booking gigs as fast as you want, or when no one has purchased your film script or TV show or paintings.

You must have a foundation so you don't falter when things get tough. You must do what others won't. Don't be the person who looks at the line and turns away.

So what are some things you can do that others might not? Implement the tools in this book. You will be far ahead of those who don't know them or don't implement them. We are living in a new world artistically.

Here's a recap of applicable steps you can take right now:

1. **Create a newsletter to market yourself.** This is more commonly done these days among artists, but

it's by no means commonplace. I've suggested this to countless artists as a way to promote, and I would venture a guess that less than 1% of them actually do it. It's very easy and there are companies that will provide you the platform for *free*. MailChimp and Constant Contact are a couple. For higher-end work you have ActiveCampaign and InfusionSoft/KEAP.

2. **Find unique ways to contact decision-makers in your field**. For me this would include casting offices, producers, directors, CEOs of production companies, and promoters. For others such as a photographers, fashion designers, or for fine artists, you'd be looking for galleries or distributors. Also find ways to connect with audience members and those people who want to buy your art, hear you sing, and so on. The goal is to make *money* because you need it to survive. And say this to yourself: "It's okay to make money." I don't know why, but from my experience artists have a hard time with that concept. Say it out loud again: *It is okay to make money*.

3. **Bypass the normal actions by contacting those in power**. What I mean by this is if you want to be in film then reach out directly to the producers and directors of those films. Send things to their offices. At the end of the day they are the ones making the decisions on casting. The producers and directors are the people in control. Casting directors are important, but their job is to help the producers and directors by pre-screening actors *before* they get to the producers. They make the early decisions on who the producers and directors should see. If you go the extra mile and make a positive impres-

sion on the producer, then you are already ten steps ahead of those who have not.

4. **Build your audience (list)** to a point where it doesn't matter if someone will cast you, hire you, put your work in a gallery, produce your film, etc. because *you* are in control and with the click of a single button on your phone or keyboard you can reach potentially thousands if not millions of people with your art. You are taking step 2 and applying it here. You are bypassing the normal way "things are done" and taking the bull by the horns.

5. **Create something.** This is the best way I have found to make yourself known and actually gives you something to promote in steps 1, 2, and 3 above. Create a concert, a show, do a reading of a script, get together with other people in your field and *do* something that will put you out there in the public eye. Create online courses, online lessons, concerts, downloads. Almost everything you can do live you can do virtually these days. The interaction is different, but you're still getting your art out there, and you're not limited to selling tickets or products to the people in close proximity to you. You can reach the entire world!

6. **Promote the heck out of it** using your lists, contacts, newsletters, social media, posters—anything you can do to get word out.

CREATE SOMETHING

This is my favorite chapter. This is the reason you will sink or swim in life.

One of my good friends is a talented marketer and artist. He said something to me that was so simple yet so impactful: "Why do actors audition? Why don't they just create the thing they want to do themselves?"

I've heard it a million times, "Easier said than done." Not true. You've set your sights on one of the most difficult professions in the world. Why go through the trials and tribulations if you weren't up for the challenge?

If you create it, build it, and grow it, then you will become that which you were previously hoping others would "make" you. You should be the puppeteer of your own life. You should be the one pulling the strings, not someone else.

Life is a continual creation. Things cannot stay in a neutral point—eventually something will move one way or the other. Sink or swim. It's really just a law of nature. Create a building and if you don't continually create (repair, build, work on), that building will, in time, eventually decay and crumble. There are examples all around you. The same is true for industry. Look at cities that once thrived and now sit in decay and poverty. This is due to an inability or refusal to grow/change with the times and create based on what is happening in the present.

Another great example is the Kodak company. Easily once the dominating force in the photography world, they were the largest provider of film for the industry. But what happened? Digital cameras were born. Kodak simply did not change with the times and therefore didn't stay relevant. They were left behind in the dust. This same thing can happen to you as a person, a spouse, significant other, worker, actor, dancer, accountant, artist, and so on. You *must* continually create to keep things relevant and current, otherwise you run the risk of becoming stagnant. Eventually stagnant things decay.

Your life, your future, and your happiness are all in *your* hands. You are solely responsible for what occurs in your life. I know it might seem odd, but it's true. How you respond to any given situation is up to you. You can choose to be happy, sad, angry, whatever. What you do with those responses makes the difference in your life and those around you.

Everything I've covered in the previous chapters culminates here. You need to create something in your life in order for it to move forward. By creating something you are taking control of your life and not "waiting for lightning to strike" or waiting "to be discovered." By creating you are pushing the momentum forward in your life. You can create a show, a dress, a photograph, a script, a marriage, a friendship, a business, and even create a better outlook on life. The world will see the energy you create, the action you take, and eventually see the product or products you create in relation to that action. This is what will set you apart from others who are sitting in stasis, waiting.

Although I have given you some examples in previous chapters, I can't tell you what to create because that is ultimately up to you. It is *your* creation. It is *your* vision. What you identify is a personal choice based on your skill set, your situation, your profession, and ultimately what you want to do. What I can do is point you in a direction, give you a road map and some survival tools, and say START!

When you take the bull by the horns and create, you are in fact manifesting your own destiny. You are not leaving things up to chance, you are not waiting for someone else to do it for you, because that will never happen.

Remember, *action creates traction*. By taking action in your life you'll eventually start to create traction, and this traction is what propels you forward. Identifying the "thing" you want to create starts with taking action. I have a program called The Hidden Artists Bootcamp where I guide participants through an in-depth look at their lives to find the artist within. The participants are made up of people from all walks of life and all professions. The truth is that each of us has an artist inside. You are the painter of the canvas that is your life. You hold the brush, choose the colors, and choose how to put those colors on the canvas. It doesn't matter what you do in life, each of us is creating our lives on a day-to-day, minute-by-minute, second-by-second basis. This becomes abundantly clear to my Bootcamp participants. It also becomes clear to them that once they unleash their hidden artist they can truly create the life they want.

They are following the Artist's Survival Guide to prosperity, and so can you.

EPILOGUE
DESTINY?

Other people have always been interesting to me. I've lost more than a few jobs because when a role presented itself, I would often recommend someone else who I felt was better suited for the role than me. My mother once asked me why I always did this. "You're taking away an opportunity for yourself," she would say. In her mind, by suggesting someone else for the role I was making it more difficult for me to get the job myself. I was creating competition for myself. My answer to her was simple: "To me they're better for the role." I like to help people. Doing so makes me feel good. I find enjoyment in the success of others and when I've helped, even in some small way, it's an incredible reward.

I'll share a story with you that changed my perspective on this business in about thirty seconds. I was on tour in the ensemble with my first big show and I had gotten a call from my agent about auditioning for a Broadway musical. This was a very successful show that had been running for a couple of years. I was so wide-eyed and excited about life. I mean, come on! I was living the dream. I was a working professional actor surrounded by like-minded artists all creating something that inspired and uplifted people. So on this day that I remember so vividly, I was standing on the loading dock of the theatre in which we were performing, talking to my agent on a payphone. This was pre-cell phones (yeah it was *that* long ago). As I was finishing the call, one of the other actors who had a leading role in the show came up to me and asked who I was talking to. This person was (and still is) a friend.

I'm not sure whether he knew it or not, but I looked to him as a "big brother" of sorts. We would talk about life and the business. He would encourage me to keep following my dreams and warn me of things to look out for on the journey. I trusted him and confided in him about my dreams, goals, and life. So, given our friendship, when he asked me who I was speaking to I told him about the audition. I was very excited because it was for a big, successful Broadway show, and I would be auditioning for the second male lead. This really could take my career to the next level. My fellow actor congratulated me on the audition and wished me good luck, for which I thanked him. I walked away feeling wonderful and supported by my friend. "What a great group of people we have in this industry," I thought. "We are all artists, working together to create something special."

A as I walked away I realized I had left my sunglasses on the top of the payphone, so I returned to grab them. As I turned the corner onto the loading dock I could hear my actor friend talking…on the payphone…telling the person on the other end about me and my audition for the big show in New York. I wasn't sure at first why he was sharing my story with someone. Was the person on the other end someone I knew? Probably not. I was a little confused until I heard him go into a pitch to have the person on the other end get him an audition for the same role, in the same show I had just told him about. He was talking to his agent. He used the information I had offered about myself to get into the audition himself.

At that moment I was stung. I was hurt. I thought, "Wow, he knows how much I want this role and he is trying to take it for himself." Questions raced through my head such as, "Is that friendship? What if he gets the role? He has more credits than I do. What if they cancel my audition to make room for him? Why did he do that? My mind was reeling with thoughts, which turned into doubts, which turned into anger, which turned into insecurity. Could I ever have the kind of friendship with this person I thought I once had? Could I confide in him? Could I trust him? Was he sharing other things I've shared with him about my life and my family?

I went back to rehearsal, finished for the afternoon and returned to my hotel where I sat and thought. In thirty seconds my viewpoint on this industry shifted. There was no place for anger, and although it would take a while for me to overcome it, there was no place for insecurity. There was only room for focus, perseverance, and success. Not just my success…everyone's success.

I remember thinking I needed to change how I was approaching this industry and my life. I remember my college drama teacher challenging us with taking greater responsibility as artists. He once said to us, "What audacity do you have to stand on a stage in front of 1,500 people and ask them to pay $100 a ticket to sit and watch you for two hours at a time?" He was daring us to look more deeply into *why* we were doing what we were doing—to move past the vanity of "being liked" and delve into the realm of responsibility for our craft, for our art, and for our lives.

So that day sitting in my hotel room I made a promise to myself—a promise I would seek to help as much as I could, to remove vanity from the equation, and instead I would try, as best I could, to take responsibility not just for myself but for those who sought out similar goals and dreams. I made a promise to myself that day, and although it has been difficult at times and at times I've faced challenges and have faltered, I've tried my best to stay true to that promise. I never told my friend about that day or how I overheard him on the phone. Instead, I pressed forward, helped when I could, and listened as much as possible. He remains a dear friend to this day.

Two weeks after that payphone call I did end up auditioning for that big show, but I didn't land the part. However, a full twenty-three years later I would go on to play the starring role, the title character in that same show for nearly three years. Life is funny that way.

I wrote this book to help, to give you some guiding steps I never had, to show you some insights into things I had to learn the hard way, and to hopefully shed light on things you might never before have thought of in terms of building your career as an artist.

I hope it helps, I hope you reach your dreams and your goals. I would only ask you this: When you do achieve your dreams and goals, reach out and help others do the same.

Keep an open mind, do the work, take chances, and be a good person. You never know how things will turn out.

The choice is yours.

Your destiny is waiting.

ABOUT THE AUTHOR

JAMES BARBOUR spent nearly three years starring as The Phantom in Broadway's longest-running smash hit musical, *The Phantom of The Opera*. An award-winning Broadway star, and international concert artist, James won the LA Ovation Best Actor Award for his portrayal of Jean Valjean in *Les Miserables* and was nominated for the Drama Desk, Drama League, and Outer Critics Awards for Best Actor in a Musical for his portrayal of Sydney Carton in the Broadway musical version of *A Tale of Two Cities*. He also won the Sarasota Magazine Best Actor Award for the Asolo Rep pre-Broadway production. He has starred on Broadway in such Tony Award-winning shows as Stephen Sondheim's *Assassins*, Disney's *Beauty and the Beast* as The Beast, *Carousel* as Billy Bigelow, *Urinetown* as Officer Lockstock, and as Edward Rochester in *Jane Eyre* (Drama League Award nomination). He also appeared in the Broadway production of *Cyrano* and the national tour of *The Secret Garden*.

His CD *Bring Me Giants* is available on iTunes and his voice can be heard on the international recording of *A Tale of Two Cities*, the PS Classics Grammy Award-nominated recording of *Assassins*, the Sony Classical cast recording of *Jane Eyre*, as well as *The Gift* on Geffen Records, Frank Wildhorn's *Dracula*, and the live CD recording of his self-produced stage show *Broadway in Concert* (for which he won an *LA WEEKLY* Garland Award). As a voice over artist

James' voice is represented on Nat Geo and Nat Deo Wild, as well as various commercials and audio books.

His television credits range from *Elementary* to the pilots of *The District*, *Just Shoot Me*, and *Flashpoint* to appearances on *Sex and the City*, *Ed*, *That's Life*, *Some Enchanted Evening: Celebrating Oscar Hammerstein* (PBS), *Beauty and the Beast: A Concert on Ice* (CBS), the PBS mini-series *American Experience: John & Abigail Adams* (playing Thomas Jefferson), and the film version of *A Tale of Two Cities* for public television.

Film credits include *Alchemy* (Tribeca Film Festival and ABC Family) starring opposite Tom Cavanagh and Sarah Chalke; Adam Sandler's *Eight Crazy Nights*, *Waiting for Lefty*, *The Tell-Tale Heart*, and *Twinkle Toes* with Sally Kirkland.

As an author and producer, James is responsible for creating many international concert series, including *James Barbour: The Holiday Concert*, *James Barbour: Love Songs*, and *Back from Broadway/Broadway in Concert* (the latter in conjunction with Steinway Concert Artist Hershey Felder). He is currently developing another one man show *The Ghosts of The Majestic* and a feature film called *Good Enough: The Ted McGrath Story*.

Mr. Barbour is considered one of the most sought-after performers on Broadway today. He is on the A-list of actors asked to develop new works for the industry's leading writers and composers including Elton John, Bernie Taupin, Frank Wildhorn, and Christopher Durang, to name a few. Mr. Barbour is also a member of the Artists' Committee of The Actors Fund.

As a motivational, keynote speaker, and seminar host, he uses his 39-plus years of experience in the entertainment world to teach others how to unleash the star power within themselves and in business and how to effectively communicate from the stage.

Website: www.jamesbarbour.com
Social Media: @JamesBarbourNow

NOTES

[1] Pressfield, Steven (2003). *The War of Art: Break Through the Blocks and Win Your Inner Creative Battles*. New York, NY: Warner Books.

[2] See https://www.nature.com/articles/s41467-019-10213-0

[3] See https://actorsequity.org/aboutequity/annualstudy/2016-2017-annual-study.pdf

[4] Cardone, Grant (2016). *The Millionaire Booklet: How to Get Super Rich*. Aventura, FL: Cardone Enterprises.